A Happy Pocket Full of
MONEY

EXPANDED STUDY EDITION

EXPANDED STUDY EDITION

A Happy Pocket Full of

MONEY

Infinite Wealth and Abundance
in the Here and Now

DAVID CAMERON GIKANDI

Cover design by Jim Warner
Cover art by Poppies, 1998 (w/c on paper), Christie, Maylee (Contemporary Artist)
/ Private Collection / Bridgeman Images
Interior design by Dutton & Sherman

Hampton Roads Publishing Company, Inc.
Red Wheel/Weiser
65 Parker Street, Suite #7
Newburyport, MA 01950-4600
Distributed by Red Wheel/Weiser, LLC
www.redwheelweiser.com

Library of Congress Cataloging-in-Publication Dat is available upon request.
ISBN: 978-1-57174-736-5

SSI

15 14 13 12

Printed on acid-free paper in the United States of America

Originally published in 2008 by Xlibris, ISBN: 978-1-4363-7166-7 (hardcover) and
978-1-4363-7165-0 (paperback).

There is a science of getting rich, and it is an exact science, like algebra or arithmetic. There are certain laws which govern the process of acquiring riches, and once these laws are learned and obeyed by anyone, that person will get rich with mathematical certainty.

—Wallace D. Wattles

CONTENTS

FOREWORD

by Bob Doyle, featured teacher in "The Secret" and
author of *Follow Your Passion, Find Your Power*

Long before I was known for my work with the Law of Attraction through "The Secret" movie or my online programs, I—like many—was a seeker. I was desperately trying to find a way to make my life better.

I was highly intrigued with a concept I had stumbled across that suggested we as human beings can somehow "create our reality"—that there were ways to be *intentional* about what our experience of life is!

Over the course of many years, I read countless books and listened to hours and hours of audio programs that explored these concepts. I read about visualization and meditation. In fact, many of the books I read were considered metaphysical or New Age. While I have nothing at all against New Age material, there was a very strong part of me that needed more than just concepts that sounded good.

I needed proof.

It wasn't that I didn't believe what I was reading. On a conscious level, I totally understood *how* using tools like visualization and meditation could somehow change the circumstances of my life.

However, I couldn't seem to make them work, which was extremely frustrating.

I had studied all of this for so long, in fact, that I became interested in teaching these principles to others. I created audio programs and did some speaking in hopes of making a living showing people how to create their lives by design.

The trouble, of course, was that I was not yet fully doing that myself. There were missing pieces to the puzzle that I still needed before I could take my intellectual understanding of these ideas and put them into practice in a way that would see results.

As a result, I was not very successful—although to this day, I believe what I was teaching was accurate. However, there were missing pieces—pieces I first needed to find for myself before I could ever make a profound difference in the lives of others.

Things became so financially bad that I finally realized that what I needed to do was just stop *trying* so hard. I had been teaching people that the "universe" would do all the figuring out for you, if you would only let it. The truth was, however, that I didn't really understand *how* that worked!

In essence, I decided to follow what I was teaching to other people, which was to listen to and act on my intuition. This meant getting clear on what I wanted in my life, and then watching for signs, if you will, of what I should do next. This was tricky at first, because the things I was led to do didn't seem to make any logical sense in terms of my goals. Still, I followed those nudges, which led me down a path that changed my life forever.

Sparing you all the details, a series of inspired conversations and "chance meetings" led me to find *A Happy Pocket Full of Money* by David Cameron Gikandi. Back then, the book was only available as an e-book (downloaded from the Internet), and when I read the promotional material about the topics covered, I was more than just a little excited. The promises of the book seemed to address every question and challenge I had with this whole "create your reality" thing, and I immediately got a copy and read it voraciously.

My mind was totally blown on many levels, because the book literally filled in *all* the blanks for me. It addressed what I hadn't even realized that I needed—the *science!*

For the first time, I was able to understand the real power of my thoughts and beliefs—that they were *real energy* that had a significant impact on my experience of life. Through reading this book, I was able to see clearly that, although I was taking a lot of action in my efforts to become successful, my true beliefs about money and success were that "money is hard to come by, and there will never be enough," because that had always been my experience growing up. I suddenly understood the power that these beliefs were having over my ability to be, do, and have all the things I wanted in life.

The book addressed the topic of quantum physics in a way that actually made sense and was easy to understand. Suddenly, creating your own reality didn't seem New Age anymore; in fact, it is something that we are all doing every moment of every day.

In what seemed like an instant, I had absolute clarity about the next steps to take in my life and how to evolve my vision for helping people to understand these concepts in a way that would make a powerful difference for them.

I immediately envisioned an online program through which I could share David's work with the world, and I contacted him to ask if he would allow me to include his book in our "Wealth beyond Reason Program" (which, by the way, was inspired by his book and would never have been created without it!).

I am eternally grateful that he agreed.

Since that time, I have had the privilege of sharing *A Happy Pocket Full of Money* with thousands of people and watching it have a similar impact on them. Eyes were opened all over the world because of David's amazing ability to communicate how the universe really works and how to utilize this knowledge practically to live amazing magical lives.

My success, my career, the differences I've been able to make in the lives of others, and the incredible opportunities I've had (like appearing in "The Secret") are all due to David Cameron Gikandi and this amazing book you hold in your hands. I consider David a friend and one of the few people I actually think of as a mentor and a hero.

This is like no other personal-development book I have ever read.

A Happy Pocket Full of Money is going to rock your world.

Have fun!

CHAPTER 1

Money: An Illusion—A Shadow of Something Else

T HE FIRST STEP TO HAVING WEALTH is to know what it is. And few people know what it really is, in and of itself. What is wealth? What causes it? What causes the cause of it? Let us start with money, the world's symbol of wealth, and then move deeper.

Money is not real.

Money is merely legal tender, a form of exchange. We use it to exchange value. It represents value.

Money is the "body" of value. It is the physical representation of value that rises and falls in ourselves, within us. Not within "things" outside of us, but within us. For without us, what is the value of a thing, such as a car? Nothing, at least not to us. In other words, it is we, the observers, that place value in things, but this value is really value in us—we give value to the material things. The material things have no "money" value in themselves—we give that to them. So money is the external physical representation of a particular section of our internal value, within us, within you. That is why a house or a block of shares valued at $1 million today can fall to a valuation of half a million dollars tomorrow when fear is introduced into the hearts of those involved. The fear kills a portion of the internal values of the participants, and that is reflected by the paper money, the "body" of value.

Here is something else: physical paper money does not even represent money in full. It cannot reasonably do that. By some estimates (and this varies from nation to nation), only as little as 4 percent of the money in the banks exists in physical form. Imagine how much cotton, linen, pulp, and metal the world would need to make all the money everyone has in his or her bank accounts. Imagine how much space it would take to store all that money as paper or coin.

If you were to stack only one million US dollar bills, it would weigh one ton and be 361 feet high. Neither does money exist as gold reserves anymore, for exactly the same reason—we ran out of the reasonable ability to maintain a gold standard in the 1970s.

So what does it exist as, the money that we are always talking about? Well, it is one massive illusion. It is all just numbers written on paper and computer storage devices and assigned to people and entities like companies and investment groups—or, more accurately, further illusion! To put it in another way, for every $100 or its equivalent in any other currency, only about $4 exists as printed paper notes or coins, while the remaining $96 exists as numbers stored on papers and computers in banks and businesses and other entities. The only reason this system does not collapse is that we all believe in it. The last time people stopped believing in it to any great extent was just before the Great Depression when large numbers of people rushed to their banks to withdraw their money and found that they could not all get it. This is not what caused the Great Depression, but it, in a large way, accelerated it.

So money is not real—something else is. Money is just the shadow of that other something. The first step to wealth is to know what money really is or, more accurately, what it represents. Learn not to look at money most of the time. As you will soon see, it is very rare that you should ever look at money as you know it today—the cash, the bank accounts, the costs, etc. This is merely the shadow and not the real thing. As you will soon see, looking at the shadow, the physical money, is mostly very unwise and unhealthy for you and your finances.

Look, instead, at the value within you and within people, and the flowing and exchanging of this value between people. Our internal value is what creates money. Money is the shadow of our internal value. Develop this internal value in yourself and in others, and your external money and wealth will rise correspondingly—automatically and without fail.

Know this however: Money represents an aspect of a person's internal value, but that does not mean that it represents a person's entire internal value. That is very important. It is not about self-worth. Money only represents an aspect of that internal value that pertains to wealth. You cannot, therefore, say that a wealthy person has a higher self-worth and value than a poor person. But you can correctly say that, in matters that relate and pertain to money, a wealthy person has a higher internal value in that aspect of value, or chooses to exercise a higher proportion of this internal value. The section of internal value that reflects on the outside as money, when exercised, is called *wealth consciousness*. It is available to all people equally and can be developed by and within all people equally. Like everything else that is important to our being alive—like air—wealth consciousness is free to all. But you can choose to develop it or not, or to exercise it or not. At any time, you can change your choice, and nothing outside of you can stop you.

You require nothing outside of yourself to increase your wealth consciousness and, therefore, your money. All you need is within you right now. You may have forgotten it, but it is right there. You will now remember it. The first step is always to remember that money is not real; it is the shadow of something else.

And here is another secret: Wealth consciousness is simply the expansion of your consciousness and awareness into the wealthy parts of your Self. That is why all you need to increase your wealth consciousness is within you already. You are already wealthy, but you have been taught to choose not to experience your wealth. This insight changes everything. Like wealthy people, you can now know how to start experiencing the wealthy you—and choose to do so.

You have more wealth capability within you than you can possibly experience in a lifetime. You need not worry that you have reached your limit of becoming wealthy in any way or because of any condition. Nor do you need to know how to convert wealth consciousness into paper money; as you will see, it will happen automatically. All you need to do is expand your wealth consciousness and exercise it, act on it, be it, and the situations and opportunities for the equivalent conversion into cash will present themselves automatically to you. None of the extremely wealthy people today could have, at the time when they were not wealthy, possibly predicted and planned the exact sequence of events that would lead to their immense wealth. They most probably had a set of goals and a plan, but any one of them will tell you that they met countless "coincidences" and opportunities that "joined the dots" for them in ways they could never have predicted. Their goals were their own doing, but the paths that led them to accomplish and exceed those goals were amazingly intelligent yet unforeseen. You shall now see how to make them happen in your life. You may not be able to predict their sequence, but you can certainly make these "fortunate coincidences" happen to you every day of your life.

By the way, it is not only paper money that is not real. A lot of the things around you that you hold to be real are not really real at all.

You are about to embark on a beautiful, empowering, and liberating journey that will show you exactly what your world is, so you can see it in a way that you have never seen it before. It is a journey that will open your eyes and free your wings. You are about to look "under the hood" of life; you are about to learn how to customize your world to your liking.

You are about to attain wealth consciousness. Once you do, avoiding success and wealth will become very difficult. Yes, you read that correctly. Once you have wealth consciousness, it will be very difficult for you *not* to have success and wealth. Success and wealth will follow you automatically wherever you go. You will not need to concern yourself with looking for them; they will find *you*. You will be free to experience other aspects of life that you may not even have dreamt of before—dimensions of self and life that are truly amazing. The same is true for happiness, for you will see it here in this book as well.

Let's get started now on the real stuff, if you are still interested.

The Steps to Wealth and Happiness

You are now on a journey, at the end of which you shall know how to create all the wealth and happiness you ever wished for—Now—without any limits. You shall soon also know many timeless truths about who you really are, what you are doing here, and what this game of life is all about. Here are the steps of the journey you are now taking with this book:

- You shall first take a simplified look at quantum physics, for knowing what you and the world are made of is the first step toward knowing how to make it work your way. After this, you will never look at the world in the same way again. You shall have an amazing sense of involvement and power in the universe.

- Then the secrets of time shall be unveiled, beginning with the fact that time does not exist. You shall learn how to use this illusion instead of being used by it. There is only Now.

- Then you will learn how to create your universe out of the quantum field using images of your mind. This is the first part of the creation lessons.

- Next, you will learn how to create using your thoughts. You will learn the right way to think, and what the mind is really for, and when to shut it down for your own benefit.

- You will then look at the power of true goal-setting in a way you may never have heard before—a most powerful way.

- Next will come the most powerful creation tool of all, your state of *Being*.

- The final creation tool, action, will then be uncovered in its true position and purpose to you.

- You shall then learn the magical and vital ingredient of certainty and learn how to have it in abundance.

- Then, it will be time to look at the prime law of the universe and how to use it to have happiness and wealth in abundance. This is the law of cause and effect.

- While still in this law, we shall look at what conditions really are. This will shock you, make you laugh, empower you, and free you.

- While still on conditions, you shall see how you are and shall realize ever-present success and never fail.

- Then you shall look at a prime killer of wealth and happiness and learn how to avoid it completely.

- You will then move on to progressively larger things. You will start with your self-chosen purpose here on earth. Why did you come here? You shall see.

- Then the gift of giving and the gifts it brings in return will be fully given to you.

- The power of gratitude Now shall be unveiled. This will prove to be extremely powerful for you.

- Finally, it will be time to look at consciousness, what makes you awake Here and Now.

- And then it will get really interesting when you have a look at your Self, the First Cause of all that is in your world. Get familiar with your Self, and your world will change dramatically.

- After that, you shall see what is larger than the Self—that of which you and all else are a part. It is the One. Knowing how you relate to All That Is, the Source, then experiencing this will put you in a position of immense joy and abundance.

- And on that note, you shall see how abundant you really are.

- From there, you will look at your real nature and how to reclaim it. It is the nature of pure joy.

- Then coming around full circle, you shall see how best to handle paper money, as you know it now, to increase wealth.

- And to close this part of the journey, you will be guided into the next empowering steps you may wish to take after you first finish this book.

How to Read and Understand This Book

The way to understand this book is to read it once in its entirety. As you read, you will have many questions, and some things may not make sense to you when you read them. Never mind; just keep going. Subsequent chapters will make clear some things that you may have not understood or found true in earlier chapters. Language is a linear thing, yet wealth consciousness is wholeness—a nonlinear whole in which step 1 may be connected to step 7 and so on. And wealth consciousness is a state of being, while language is a symbol. States have to be experienced, and symbols cannot represent experience accurately. They can only show the way, be a guide. So as you read this book, you will find many amazing things that make sense right then, but it will only make complete sense when you have finished it and have the whole of it in you. That is when you will start to say, "Aha!"

Once you have read the book fully, read it again slowly. In the second read, you will be able to understand things more fully, since you now will have the whole in you. The material you will find in this book contains many layers of understanding. What you understand today will reveal an even deeper hidden truth, application, and identification when you read it again tomorrow. Read a small part of this book every day, even after you finish it the first time, and your internalization of wealth and happiness and your becoming wealthy and happy will accelerate.

Don't read this book with your logical mind; feel the lessons in this book. Some of the things in this book are logical, but many pertain to a realm that logic cannot fully grasp. Yet your Self knows it all and perfectly understands. As you read this book, keep yourself open, feel the essence of what you read. Many things will not make sense to your brain, for it is finite and four-dimensional. Some things are infinite and multi-dimensional. Only your Self will know them because it is multi-dimensional and infinite in nature. Sometimes you will feel that you understand something at a deeper level—your mind may not be able to picture it, yet you understand it deeply somewhere. Honor the deeper level, for your mind may never fully grasp it anyway. In any case, your mind is a tool, but all you know is in your Self. You are a Self with a mind as a powerful tool, as long as it does not take you over. However, most people have unfortunately identified with their minds and believe that they are their minds—and that is where the trouble and limitations start. You shall now go higher than that.

Read this book and take it to heart. Live by it, and wealth, affluence, and abundance will automatically come to you in ways and amounts you never before imagined possible, by laws that never fail. Carry it around with you whenever possible. Leave it by your bedside, and read it for a few minutes every morning when you get up and at night before you go to sleep. When you are done, start again, a few pages every day. Repetition causes internalization, making it your second nature.

You will understand this book to the extent that you are willing. Ready? Still interested? Let's begin.

CHAPTER 2

Quantum Physics: Know What You and the World Are Made Of

Y OU MAY BE WONDERING what quantum physics has to do with wealth and happiness. Well, you had better believe that it has everything to do with it! How can you build a house if you do not know what a house is made of and how it is constructed?

Quantum physics begins to explain how everything in your world comes to be. You are in direct control of your entire physical world, but you may not be aware of this fact. And your lack of awareness of this fact—how the physical matter comes about and your role in it—makes your life appear to you as an occurrence that is out of your control. It may appear to you as if you are the victim of circumstances, while all along you are the cause of those circumstances, including your experiencing of wealth or lack of it.

Quantum physics is the first step in an amazing awakening that you are about to undergo. Not only will you understand the very construction of all that you see around you, you will also understand exactly how your belief and thinking creates matter, how you reap what you sow, how "even before you ask, it has been given unto you." It is science finally catching up with spirituality and common sense, and explaining it! Think about it; when someone tells you that anything is possible if only you believe, aren't you more likely to believe that when you know how, step-by-step and scientifically, your belief shifts the universe and produces what you believe in?

One of the benefits of understanding the very basics of quantum physics (and the basics is all you need to understand) is that you finally see clearly how powerful concepts like faith and right thinking work. This seeing and understanding, this knowing, enables you to have full confidence, eliminate doubt, and create your reality consciously, powerfully, and beautifully—and in many ways, become more powerful.

Quantum physics also shows you how we are all connected, how we are all One Being that perpetuates an illusion of separate individual beings. It also gives you a glimpse into how spirit and matter connect, how mind and matter interact, how creation actually happens, and how we are co-creators with God. By the end of this chapter and the next four chapters, you will be amazed at how much power you have, how amazing this universe is, and how easy it is to create any outcome you choose.

But first, what is quantum physics? Quantum physics is the study of the building blocks of the universe. For example, your body is made up of cells. These cells are, in turn, made up of molecules, which are made up of atoms, which are, in turn, made up of subatomic particles like electrons. This is the world of quantum physics. Everything is made up of "large groups" of subatomic particles. Your body, a tree, thoughts, a vehicle, a planet, light, and everything else are "concentrations" of energy. All of them are large collections of pretty much the same types of subatomic particles. The only difference is in the way these particles are grouped together into ever-larger building blocks. Knowing how they work is a key to knowing how to recreate yourself and the world around you.

To speak correctly, a subatomic particle is not really a particle in the way that a grain of sand is a particle. While atomic and larger particles are objects, or things, subatomic particles are not objects as such. They are "probabilities of existence" and, at the same time, "multiple existences." They are also wave-like and particle-like at the same time. You will see what all this means by the end of this chapter.

Quantum physics asks the question: What are these subatomic particles and how do they act? Well, the subatomic particles are energy packets sometimes called *quanta*. Everything in this universe is made up of energy, and these energy packets behave in the most amazing way! They are at our command! The reason they arrange themselves into a luxury boat, for example, is our individual and collective thoughts. Do you now start to see the link between wealth and quantum physics? Up until this point, you may have been designing your world haphazardly and unconsciously. Now you will awaken and do it deliberately and consciously with direction.

Journey into the Quantum Field

What is your body made of? Tissues and organs. What are tissues and organs made of? Cells. What are cells made of? Molecules. What are molecules made of? Atoms. What are atoms made of? Subatomic particles. What are subatomic particles made of? Energy? No. They are not made of energy; they *are* energy. You are one big "chunk" of energy. And so is everything else. Spirit and mind put this energy together into the physical shapes you are used to seeing.

—I am wealth. I am abundance. I am joy.—

Quantum physics tells us that it is the act of observing an object that causes it to be there, where and how we observe it. Energy is the subatomic particles that, in turn, make up atoms and, finally, matter.

This energy exists as waves spread out over space and time. Only when you exercise observation do these waves become particles localized as a space-time event—a particle at a particular "time" and "place." As soon as you withdraw observation, they become a wave again. So as you see, your observation—your attention to something and your intention—literally creates that thing as a space-time event. This is scientific. In other chapters, we shall see how to focus, concentrate, and guard your attention, intention, and thought to create your reality exactly.

—I am wealth. I am abundance. I am joy.—

No solid object is solid. It is made up of rapidly flashing packets of energy. Billions and trillions of packets of energy. They flash in and flash out of that space where the "object" is. They do not just stay there. So, why does a human body or a car look like a solid continuous object when we now know that it is actually a rapidly flashing field of energy? Think of a motion-picture image. When you watch a movie, you see a person walk across the screen smoothly, yet in reality it is just a series of twenty-four slightly different frames passing before you each second so your eyes do not detect the gap between the frames. And each of those frames is a composition of billions of light photons flashing at the speed of light. That is what your world is—a rapid flash that causes an illusion of being "solid" and "continuous." Once you understand what your world really and truly is, you start to understand its true behavior and nature. You can then change your view of it. And with your changed perception, you can change your creation of it. This is the first step to wealth.

—I am wealth. I am abundance. I am joy.—

Every single physicist agrees on one thing: subatomic particles, those energy "packets" or quanta, are not particles in a particular point in space and time—like a table or a chair. They are a probability that can exist at various points in space and time. The act of us observing them converts them into a "physical" particle at a particular point in space and time, and once we withdraw that attention, they become a probability again. Imagine that the chair in your living room is one big subatomic particle. This is how it would act:

> When you are not in the house and not thinking of your chair, it would "vanish" and become a probability that it can "reappear" anywhere in your living room or anywhere else in the universe.

> When you come back home and think of sitting on a chair in a particular spot in your living room, and you look for a chair at that spot, it would magically reappear!

This is not some fantasy magical story. Subatomic particles behave just like that!

The amazing thing is that all matter is composed purely of massive amounts of these particles. Therefore, all matter acts exactly like a large group of subatomic particles would. A chair's "being there" is a result of us all watching it be there and deciding it is there. It is not a wholly independent existence. No matter has wholly independent existence independent of all observers. As some scientists say, if everyone and everything in the universe stopped looking at the moon or thinking about it, it would not be a physical moon any more—it would be a probability of existence. The act of observation makes the probability become a definite thing and all other probabilities of it being elsewhere in the same world null. Continuous attention keeps it that way, producing the illusion of a solid continuous existence of a physical moon.

—I am wealth. I am abundance. I am joy.—

Physicists have also discovered that quantum "particles" make decisions. They are powered by intelligence. Not only that, they also know, instantly, what decisions are being made by other particles any-where else in the universe! This synchronicity across space and time is instantaneous—particles "communicate" without taking any time or crossing any space. In fact, they also move instantaneously, without having to go across space or take time. They can get from point A to point B without having to cross the space in between, and point A and point B can be in different times. Remember that quantum "par-ticles" are not particles in the sense you normally think of particles. They are not "things" that are at a particular "place" and "time"—they are spread across space and time.

So what is the intelligence that powers them? Well, it is from the mind of the Source, God—all that is, proportionately made up your own "individual" mind and also the "individual minds" of the rest of the universe, depending on the subject matter, scope, and strength of will.

Think about all this carefully. Think about the fact that every-thing your eye can see is made up of these amazing particles, which are under your control. Think about the scientific facts that now prove that you are a cause, or co-cause, of everything around you, and that nothing you observe can exist without your observation. All you need to do is choose what you wish to observe—choose it with certainty and consistency—and this will cause the energy field to material-ize into that thing over "time," depending on your clarity, focus, and certainty. Scientists have discovered that, even in the strictest double-blind experiments, their expectations still influence results, and that it is impossible to carry out an experiment where there is absolutely no influence from the observer on the results of the experiment.

—I am wealth. I am abundance. I am joy.—

Quantum packets or particles are best defined as probabilities of existence. For example, say you have a quantum packet called Mr. X. Before you ask to speak to Mr. X, he will not exist as a person. He will exist as a potential person. Mr. X will be all over the world at the same time with varying potentials to appear in person in Moscow, New York, Kabul, Tokyo, Sydney, Cape Town, or any other town in the world. Now, when you call his name, he will appear where you called him; at that point, the probability of him appearing in any other city will become zero. Then, when you finish your conversation with him, he will vanish again. He will stop being a localized person, spread out like a wave, and become once again possessed of the probability of appearing anywhere in the world. That is how a quantum packet called Mr. X would behave. Keep in mind that everything in this universe is made up of quantum packets.

—I am wealth. I am abundance. I am joy.—

Another property of quanta is that they are multi-dimensional. So in the example of Mr. X, when he is a probability, he is multi-dimensional. When he localizes—when we call him—he becomes a thing in our four-dimensional world. (Our world as we know it is actually four-dimensional, with dimensions of length, width, height, and time.) This is scientific. You now see, scientifically, that our universe is multi-dimensional, although our senses are capable of detecting only the dimensions of length, width, height, and time. Yet our souls are also multi-dimensional. Listen to your soul, your feelings.

—I am wealth. I am abundance. I am joy.—

The physical world is literally made up of ideas and energy.

—I am wealth. I am abundance. I am joy.—

If you ever feel powerless, consider this: Einstein and other quantum scientists have proven that all physical matter is made up of energy packets that are not bound by space and time. This energy field has no well-defined boundaries. The universe is literally your extended timeless and unbound body. Science has also proven that the mind has no boundaries. All minds are "connected" into One Mind. You are bigger and more powerful than you think you are. So stop sweating the small stuff.

—I am wealth. I am abundance. I am joy.—

You already have it all. It has been said that, before you ask, it was already given to you. Science is beginning to prove, through quantum physics, that this is scientifically true. The infinite intelligence and potentiality at the quantum level—the level that makes up all that is around us and our inherent abilities to influence this field—is what gives us the "having it all." We are beginning to know this on a larger scale—scientifically, as well as spiritually.

You already have riches beyond your wildest dreams. You have them. You may not be experiencing them right now, but you have them. Having and experiencing are two different things. An easy way to explain it is that you have the ability to fly a plane or surf a wave or go scuba diving; but you may not have experienced this aspect of your ability. There is nothing you need to do to have this ability; it is already in you. It has already been done for you. All you need to do is experience it.

In our lives, we really are simply shifting our consciousness to experience aspects of ourselves that we have always had, in a universe that has all that we can possibly wish to have, even that which we have not imagined exists. The quantum field can form an infinite number of shapes and experiences. In fact, it has already done that. The pages of this book are just one of those things; the words you are reading are just one of those things; the next thought you will have is just one of those things. Yet you never predicted you would be experiencing these pages. But your desire to read these words has caused them to appear in your hands. Indeed, they have always existed. You need not predict exactly how things will work out; all you need to do is desire, intend, and know it's possible—and it will be arranged to come to you.

—I am wealth. I am abundance. I am joy.—

Many physicists working on subatomic particles are coming to discover several interesting things about our universe. They have, for example, found out that two particles separated by space and time can be "invisibly linked" to each other and act in synchrony. They have also found out that the world we live in appears to have been constructed in such a way that it knows itself. This appears to have been done by "cutting" the One whole into at least two states—one designed to see and one designed to be seen. The one designed to see is under the illusion that it is separated from the one that is designed to be seen. It is a necessary illusion, a persistent one. But everything is actually One.

—I am wealth. I am abundance. I am joy.—

The whole universe is brought into being by the participation or observation of those who participate and observe. Wealth is brought into existence by you and all of us looking at it. Your certainty of it, your faith in it, and your attention to it *creates* it. In reality, it already exists as a probability wave, but you now cause it to be a definite thing, an event in a point in space and time. It goes even deeper than that. It already exists as an event, but your perception of time makes it look "away" and "separate." Once you understand what time is and how it works, you will be able to bring things into your experience faster and in larger amounts.

—I am wealth. I am abundance. I am joy.—

Now, let's get a little more complicated. We have seen that subatomic particles exist as probabilities and that, when we observe them, we cause localization in a particular point in space and time. In other words, a particle has the potential of being in place A, B, C, and D. When we observe place C, it appears in place C and ceases to have the possibility of appearing in places A, B, and D, at least until we stop observing it in place C. Well, a new school of thought is studying the Everett-Wheeler-Graham theory, which says that this quanta will actually localize in all four of these points, but in different worlds that coexist with ours! In other words, all possibilities actually manifest into the physical, but in different parallel worlds! There is supporting evidence of this from physicists who are studying signs that the universe is a giant multi-dimensional hologram. How does this work? Well, when a particle has a probability to be in places A, B, C, and D, it will not choose just one place to be in; it will choose all four. But for this to be possible, the universe "splits" into four parallel worlds, each one unaware of the other three. This is called the "many worlds" interpretation of quantum mechanics.

It sounds crazy, but think about it. It is definitely possible— nothing is impossible for the Source, God. Many religions tell us that even before we ask, it is given unto us. We are also told that everything that can possibly exist exists Now. We also now know that the universe splits itself, or rather creates the illusion of separation, so that one "piece" can be the observed piece and the other "piece" can be the observer piece—and so it knows itself. The One splits itself so that it can know itself and have something with which to compare itself. For when it is only One, there is no possibility of comparison that can allow it to know what it is.

Your Self, your spirit or soul, is eternal and existing across space and time. Now, the next decision you make will split the universe. You will be conscious to the part of the universe you chose. You will also exist in the other part that you did not choose, but you will not be "awake" to it, even though its essences will still come to you and help you know that which you chose and vice versa. Other people who chose the other world you did not choose will be "awake" there and not here in your world. Now you can see how free will works without conflicting with itself, and how truths can seem to be contradictory, yet all can be true.

The universe is also "split" into your present self, your past selves, and your future selves, although you are only awake to one of those selves at a time (your present self). Thus your future selves, for example, are able to warn your present "awake" self of things they went through and did not like so that you do not go through them. It is a huge ever-shifting matrix, and a very complex one. The whole matrix shifts with every decision. Life is a pattern of eternal processes existing all at once with all possible existences—Now—and you only choose the one you will be awake to from instant to instant. Physics is only now beginning to prove this. By the way, dreaming is simply another state of consciousness. When you dream, your consciousness is in another realm, world, or time. Do you see where your dreams may be coming from now?

All this will make more sense when you understand what time is and how it works.

—I am wealth. I am abundance. I am joy.—

We now know that the entire universe came from a small sub-atomic particle-like existence and has been expanding at a rate faster than you can imagine ever since—oceans forming, worlds forming, all courtesy of quantum physics. But the truth is even more magical than that. The universe is continually giving birth to new universes. Many physicists now see evidence of this type of "many worlds" behavior, and several interpretations of quantum physics to this effect exist. Most physicists believe that this is a continuous, but chaotic or random, occurrence, largely because they have found no other reason for it. But ask yourself, what part does spirit play? What part do you play, your Self, your soul? Could your choices be the cause of this observed "chaotic" splitting of worlds? Physicists like to exclude spirit in their studies, yet spirit is what gives rise to matter and not the other way around. Think about that. Einstein is one of the few physicists who refused to believe that all this happens randomly or by chance. He said he refused to believe that "God plays dice."

—I am wealth. I am abundance. I am joy.—

Know this: the quantum world is the real world. The world you see with your eyes is simply an imperfect perception of a group of quantum activity. Yet the quantum activity is caused by you—you are First Cause. Never think that what you see with your eyes is First Cause—it is just an effect. A good illustration of this is the famous Schrödinger's Cat experiment (by Erwin Schrödinger, who was awarded the Nobel Prize in 1933). It depicts what actually is happening when you place a cat in a box with a closed bottle of poison gas, as well as a device that will open the gas bottle and thus kill the cat. You then close the box so that you cannot see inside it. The gas in the bottle, by the way, only becomes poisonous if one particular radioactive atom in the box decays. Quantum physics shows that this radioactive atom exists simultaneously in the "decayed" and the "not decayed" states, until it is measured (until you open the box to see whether the cat is dead or not). Remember, everything exists in all possible states until you observe it. You cannot know whether the cat is dead or alive without opening the box. While the box remains closed, the cat is both dead and alive at the same time. This is why quantum physics is so crazy—two contradictory states actually coexist! When you open the box to check whether that radioactive atom decayed or not—and therefore whether the cat died or not—then one of these two outcomes will materialize. Yet physicists now know that their expectations and thoughts influence results, and that the "many worlds" interpretation tells us that both actually happened, but in two separate worlds created by the choice you made.

—I am wealth. I am abundance. I am joy.—

We now know that everything in the universe is a wave-particle duality. What this means is that everything, including your body and your car, is a wave and a particle at the same time. There is no difference between you and light, except for the fact that light has a different wavelength than you do. Other than that, you are pretty much the same thing as light. And remember—it is physics telling us this now. Several thousand years ago, various spiritual teachers told us the same thing—we came from light. You are light. In fact, your body, when you examine it under a microscope, is over 99 percent "space." The rest of it, the solid part, is just a collection of the exact same things that light is made of, the same subatomic particles. Actually, even the "space" is full of energy.

Your mind, from your spirit, keeps your body "together" as a "solid" unit. And your mind does the same thing with other things around you. All matter is put together using information from your mind and the minds of those around you and the rest of the universe.

—I am wealth. I am abundance. I am joy.—

Einstein's equation $E=mc^2$ states that the energy contained in any matter is equal to the mass of that matter multiplied by the speed of light squared (and that is a very large number!). This shows you two things:

- Even the smallest tiny piece of matter has a tremendous amount of energy in it (that is how nuclear explosions happen).

- You and everything else are just energy arranged together by information from the mind.

—I am wealth. I am abundance. I am joy.—

The subatomic world is not static at all. It is an amazing dance of never-ending creation and destruction, with particles destroying themselves and—in that very destruction—giving rise to new ones. Most subatomic particles have an unimaginably short life (billionths of a second). The whole universe is forever being recreated anew. You can imagine it all being wiped clean and restored, just a little differently, every trillionth of a second or so. Okay, here is another amazing thing: when a particle is created, it is instantly traveling at the speed of light! So we did, quite literally, come from light, as many creation stories tell us. One more thing: particles can move forward and backward in time. And this is the stuff you are made of and that you control!

—I am wealth. I am abundance. I am joy.—

There is no such thing as empty space. All "space" is filled with energy—the same energy that makes up you and everything else. It is just that your five senses—sight, sound, touch, taste, and smell—do not detect the many varied types of forms that exist in the universe. In other words, you can only detect forms that are recognized by those five senses (unless you have developed other senses). But that does not mean that forms that are humanly perceptible are the only things that exist in this universe. Think of the universe as a hologram. Anyway, the whole point of this is to know that you are part of one huge ocean of energy and that literally nothing separates you from anything else. The only "separation" you see is an illusion caused by your limited five senses. Quite literally, we are all One.

We are one large organic whole whose parts are changing all the time. Each part can look at the other parts, and each part has its own level of consciousness and awareness. Yet the whole acts exactly as a whole, while the parts act as a part of the whole with individual and whole properties.

—I am wealth. I am abundance. I am joy.—

In 1964, Dr. J. S. Bell, a physicist at the European Organization for Nuclear Research (CERN) in Switzerland, came up with mathematical proof that all the "separate" parts of the universe are connected in an immediate and close way. Many experiments now show that particles separated by space and time somehow know exactly what other particles are doing at the exact time they are doing that particular thing. In other words, particles do not communicate. Communication takes time and requires a message. This is different. They *know* without having to communicate. They act *simultaneously* as if they are intimately connected somehow across space and time, in a way that is not affected by the separation in space and time between them.

—I am wealth. I am abundance. I am joy.—

The other profound thing that Bell's mathematical constructs show is that the action of a subatomic particle is dependent on something happening somewhere else to another subatomic particle. In other words, all subatomic events are effects of others and causes of others. This brings the law of cause and effect, of karma, of reaping and sowing, into a completely new light! The law of cause and effect, karma, is not only spiritual, but also scientific.

—I am wealth. I am abundance. I am joy.—

All along, we have said that all the universe's thoughts, individually and collectively, cause energy to "form" into the physical reality we experience. This is so, but there is an even stronger cause—Being, the state of Being. There are many states of being, like being happy, fast, wealthy, and so on. This is the strongest cause, the First Cause of all. It is so because it is the declaration of spirit, of Self. From a state follows certain thoughts pertaining to that state.

—I am wealth. I am abundance. I am joy.—

Here is another way of looking at how we are all one. Science shows us that everything is made up of energy and that exchanges of that energy occur at all times in a most complex way. Energy is the building block of all matter. The energy that composes your flesh is the same energy that composes the bricks of your house and the trees outside. There is no "energy of the tree" and "energy of the man." It is all the same energy. Energy is constantly in flux, changing form all the time. This is a very simple explanation of a rather complex thing.

At the quantum level, it all looks like one large pool of energy "soup"—an ocean of energy that is always flowing, and that has different concentrations and essences at various points. Imagine an ocean with a warm spot, a turbulent spot, and so on. (The ocean represents the energy "soup" and the spots represent various physical objects like your body or a tree). The warm spot exchanges water molecules with the rest of the ocean. The turbulent spot also exchanges water molecules with the rest of the ocean. But the essence of that warm spot remains warmth, and that of the turbulent spot turbulence. There is an exchange and flow on a molecular level; on the larger level, however, the spots remain warm or turbulent, even though the molecules that composed them a moment ago are gone and replaced by others from other regions. The molecules in a warm spot change, but the essence or characteristic of that spot remains warmth. The characteristics of a region can remain the same, even though the particles forming that region are always different, leaving and entering it from other regions. This is how we look on a quantum level—like one large interconnected field of energy with localizations of characteristics. We share the same energy with everything else, even though we assume unique characteristics. It is a very complex matrix, a complex web.

Now let's get a little more complicated than the ocean. Imagine now that there are two people in a room. They are both gloomy and sad. Their energy level is low. One tells a joke, and the other one laughs. The one telling the joke causes the one who starts to laugh to raise his or her energy level and become vibrant. This makes the one telling the joke laugh because there is new joy in the air, and they are sharing the joke. Person A caused a change in person B, and it went back to cause a change in person A. Now, have you noticed how you feel great after you tell jokes to a lot of people and they laugh? How it makes you feel better than telling the joke to just one person? And those people take your joke, and they tell it to other friends and to friends of friends, and so it spreads. Well, the universe is a whole lot more complicated than that. A shift on one part of that massive field of energy ripples on and causes shifts in the parts next to it, and they cause shifts in the parts next to them, and that ripple goes on forever! Can you imagine that! Your smile changes the composition of the entire universe! Scientifically! Your anger does the same.

Anything you do, any thought you have, ripples on forever and changes the composition of the whole universe, however small that change is.

Now here is something even more interesting. Because you are part of that universe, that ripple comes back to you and gives you back a dose of similar essence. You cause a change in the energy field around and in you, and it ripples, touching everything. And everything, of course, ripples back in reaction, sending it back to you, all multiplied! It is similar to the way ripples form in expanding circles when you dip your finger in a glass of calm water. But these waves go forever and also bump into other energy localizations and cause changes in them, and these react, so to speak, and send back their own waves. And these returned waves hit you and change you, and you react, and this amazing dance goes on and on. That is how, scientifically, the law of cause and effect works—multiplicatively. This happens on an energy level and on a spirit level as well. In both cases, the betterment of one individual in the system causes a betterment of the whole system, and betterment in the whole system causes betterment in the individual. The reverse is also true.

—I am wealth. I am abundance. I am joy.—

All other things held constant, to the extent that an individual or society understands what it and its universe are made of and learns how to control that creation, so will it have wealth and happiness.

That is our brief introduction into the stuff we are all made of. Do not worry if something did not make sense; it will make sense later as you go on with this book and read other related things.

You do not need to master quantum physics to be wealthy. This chapter is enough. The point of this chapter was simply to show you what your world really is and to help you realize that you are in very direct control of it. The rest of this book will show you how to exercise that control and read the feedback it gives you. But in case you wish to learn more about quantum physics specifically, please feel free to do so. To learn more about quantum physics, visit *aHappyPocket.com* for videos, articles, and book recommendations.

Quantum physics shows you that the world is not the hard and unchangeable thing it may appear to be. Instead, it is a very fluid place continuously built up using our individual and collective thoughts and states of being as individuals, a family, a society, a country, a planet, a solar system, or a universe. We have begun to uncover the illusion. We now know what our four-dimensional experiences are made of, and we have begun to see how we make them. The next step is to know what the other part of our world is, what the fourth dimension, time, really is. It is time to look at time.

CHAPTER 3

The Truth about Time:
It Does Not Exist

TIME IS A FUNNY THING. A very funny thing. The biggest trick time ever played on us was to make us think it was real, and that we were under its full control. Yet time is a complete illusion, a strong and persistent illusion.

What wonderful news that is! Time is an illusion created by you. Once you understand how this illusion is created by you, you can begin to recreate it as you wish—consciously and deliberately, instead of unconsciously and accidentally as you may have been doing.

What is time? What do I have to do with time? How should I think and be about time so that I may experience wealth and other things in larger quantities faster? This chapter will begin to answer these questions. In other chapters in this book, these concepts will become more real to you.

The only time that truly exists is Now.

The distinction between past, present and future is only an illusion, however persistent.

—Albert Einstein

—I am wealth. I am abundance. I am joy.—

Whether time is long or short, and whether space is broad or narrow, depend upon the mind. Those whose minds are at leisure can feel one day as a millennium, and those whose thoughts are expansive can perceive a small house to be as spacious as the universe.

—Hung Tzu-ch'eng

—I am wealth. I am abundance. I am joy.—

Time flows in all directions, not only forward as it appears to. The past, present, and future exist simultaneously.

—I am wealth. I am abundance. I am joy.—

Here is an easy explanation of what time is. This is an extremely simplified explanation, but it will do for now. Imagine a football or soccer field with ten objects spread around it. Now, imagine that object A represents a child being born and object B represents a ten-year-old child. If object A were to travel to (become or transform into) object B, that travel would take what you now call "ten years of time"—that is, ten human years of a child growing up. Now, it gets a little complex. What if that football field were to shrink? Object A would reach (become) object B and pass through all the experiences of ten years of childhood, but the sensation of time would change. In other words, ten years would feel very different. If the field shrank enough, ten years could feel like an instant. And you have experienced this often. When you are having a great time, you feel as if time flies by. You don't notice the hours pass, yet your watch says they passed, because your watch is designed to take the same amount of "time" to move from one second marker on the clock face to the next. But you are not designed that way. Time is the moving of your consciousness past preexisting events in the space-time continuum. You will soon see what this is.

The field of life that we live in is not static; it keeps changing its dimensions. That is why we have to keep readjusting our watches worldwide all the time for this crazy thing called time to make sense to us—but only because we think of time as consistent slices of a whole. It is not. It is merely our misinterpretation of our consciousness moving past one preexisting event in the field to the next, as you shall soon see. The field of life is not static, nor does our consciousness move at a fixed speed. The field may not change that fast for us, and our consciousness may not change its rate that fast unless we will it to do so, and that is why we do not usually notice these differences that much and realize that time is not constant.

But if you were to travel very fast in a spaceship, as you may well have heard from Einstein's Theory of Relativity, you can slow down time or even go back in time. Time is more of a sensation of passing events, and the speed with which you pass these events determines the calibration of time. It is not the taking of time that changes; it is the calibration of time (one minute no longer takes one minute).

Okay, back to the soccer field. Imagine you are one of the objects. You will feel time as you move around the field passing other objects that you see, won't you? Yes. Now, imagine if you were born moving faster—say three times the speed. Time would seem shorter. Now, imagine you are the soccer field itself! Or even an object large enough to cover the whole field. Now we are talking! Time would cease to exist for you because you are the field and you can feel, touch, and be with all the objects on it at the same time. There is no travel from one object to another; they are all happening Here, Now. All of them. All ten objects happening at the same "time" for you, always. This is the eternal moment of Now, Here. Everything that can possibly happen in the universe—everything that can possibly be created, the past, present, and future—are all running at the same "time" in one huge field. Your consciousness and awareness are awake to only a small section of this field at any one "time." And as you move objects (or events) about from one point to another, you experience "time" as a sensation of past, present, and future. The field itself does not experience time; it only experiences an eternal process that is always happening all at once—Now, Here, Always, All Ways. You can think of the whole field as the Source.

As you expand your consciousness and awareness, you take up more and more of the field and time shrinks for you. Can you see that? Now, the amazing thing is that the mind and the Self (or soul or spirit, whichever term you use) is a lot larger than your physical body. We are used to thinking of the soul or Self as a little thing contained inside our body. That is just human thinking—relating things to containers. Have you ever considered that the soul, being far more powerful than the body, actually holds the body together and surrounds it? And the mind holds the brain and nervous system together and surrounds it. If you have considered that the soul and mind are larger than the body and brain, have you ever considered where they end? How many feet away from your body? Or is it how many miles away? Or how many light years away from your body does your soul end? It is not impossible that your soul and mind are a billion times larger than your body. Why not? They are infinite and eternal. Yet this humongous powerful Self is you.

Anyway, let us get back to wealth. Understanding time clearly—how it works and how to take control of it—and understanding your Self and your Self's composition and relation with everything else physical and nonphysical is of high importance if you wish to experience massive wealth "fast." It is all a matter of expanded consciousness, right state, right thought, and right choice. These can awaken your consciousness to wealthy parts of the whole that spread out in ever-wider circles from your Self.

—I am wealth. I am abundance. I am joy.—

Now is the only moment that exists. An eternal moment of Now is all there is. You can remember the past and dream the future, but you can only *be, exist,* Here, Now. Make an irrevocable commitment to yourself to make Now the best moment of your life ever!

—I am wealth. I am abundance. I am joy.—

Do not dwell in the past or live in the future. Your only moment is Now. Dwell in Now.

—I am wealth. I am abundance. I am joy.—

As you will soon see, your outer world mirrors your inner world. You will see in this book how this is so.

Do you feel as if you do not have enough time to do what you wish to do? People short of time on the outside are short of it on the inside. They act, think, and speak from a belief that they are short of time. Stop thinking and saying you do not have enough time. Do not believe that for a second. The universe has no shortages of anything—including time—and neither do you. The only limitations or shortages are those that you build for yourself. Believing in any sort of shortage makes your consciousness smaller and slower so that you may experience what you believe in.

—I am wealth. I am abundance. I am joy.—

The present moment is the greatest gift you can have. It is perfectly created for you according to your stated designs. You state these designs by the thoughts, states of being, words, and actions that you held most true to yourself earlier. The present is something that you send yourself, a perfectly pre-sent moment. It allows you to experience, taste, review, and change your past thoughts, states of being, words, and actions. Be grateful for the present, for you know you can change it. It allows you to experience your Self, for its entire existence is to serve you. Cursing, condemning, and judging the present moment will only keep it as it is longer. What you resist, judge, and condemn persists. What you embrace and bring to the light for non-judgmental, honest, and clear examination reveals the lessons you are looking for—the key to the next level you seek.

—I am wealth. I am abundance. I am joy.—

Time is only an illusion produced by the succession of our states of consciousness as we travel through eternal duration, and it does not exist where no consciousness exists in which the illusion can be produced; but "lies asleep."

—H. P. Blavatsky

—I am wealth. I am abundance. I am joy.—

The future influences the present just as much as the past.

—Friedrich Nietzsche

—I am wealth. I am abundance. I am joy.—

The first time you do something is always a journey of discovery. You take in the details and learn many new things. At this point, there are no labels and memories to enable you to prejudge the new experience. Learning is at its highest. The hundredth time you do something, it is often a very different experience. For most people, repetition brings about unconsciousness. Most people do and see the things that occur most often in their lives in an unconscious and unaware state. Because they have seen or done them before, they turn to relying on their memories and on labels they built in their minds the first time they had the experience. Learning and discovery drops to zero. Memories of past experiences take over. But what good does it do to live today based on your memory of yesterday? You miss the gift of the present moment totally! In your business or work, do you take an absolutely fresh look at your work, workmates, and customers each new day? Or do you go by how you "knew" them in their past?

Everything changes, and using memory keeps you from seeing that change, seeing things as they truly are. Try to "forget" everything about what you are looking at, and you will discover a whole new world. You will grow a whole lot faster, and grow your wealth and self a whole lot quicker.

Think about it. How often does a stranger complement your workmate or spouse about something that you totally miss every day because you do not look at them as if they were totally new to you? Memory has its place, but many people overuse it—and often in a non-beneficial way.

Decide right now to face every experience anew by choosing to forget that you have ever faced it before. Decide not to anticipate a specific appearance or behavior based on your memory and emotions. When you practice detachment but are sure of your choices and intention, you will find a world that has been hiding from you all along—right in front of your eyes, all along.

—I am wealth. I am abundance. I am joy.—

Choose happiness, present-moment living, and joy at all times. Thank the present moment for all it brings you in enjoyable experiences—for the opportunities it gives you to see yourself as you were before and to grow to an even greater self.

—I am wealth. I am abundance. I am joy.—

Bring into the present moment your awareness, consciousness, thoughts, and "looking." Life and all your opportunities to move forward are in the present, the ever-present moment of Now, Here.

—I am wealth. I am abundance. I am joy.—

Do not "throw" yourself forward into where you wish to be all day long. Imagination about the future is great, for it is what you use to create your future. But the present has great value. Only through acting and living in the present can you get to the future. Do not spend all day daydreaming about a future time—saying "if only," mentally escaping your present and dwelling in an imaginary tomorrow, going about the whole day in a dreamlike state, being only half aware and conscious of the details going on in your day. These behaviors actually slow you down on your trip to a better tomorrow. Just as it is necessary to set future goals if you wish to progress, it is necessary to embrace and experience the present and act in it consciously and with awareness. Remember, the universe can only use the present moment to send you clues, people, events, and opportunities to advance; it cannot use the imaginary future in your head. Instead of chasing a better life by throwing your consciousness into the future, bring it back to the present and let the future chase it there.

—I am wealth. I am abundance. I am joy.—

Now, Here.

—I am wealth. I am abundance. I am joy.—

A Happy Pocket Full of Money

The wheels of time are mysterious. Time is a concept of mind. Without mind, there is no concept of time. Annihilate the mind. You will go beyond time. You will enter the realm of Timeless. You will live in the Eternal.

—*Swami Sivananda*

—I am wealth. I am abundance. I am joy.—

Do not dwell in the past. Do not dream of the future. Concentrate the mind on the present moment.

—*Buddha*

—I am wealth. I am abundance. I am joy.—

Be careful how you set deadlines for yourself. Time does not exist as an absolute. Quantum physics, our spirituality, and our understanding of eternity all tell us that the only time that truly exists is Now, and the only place is Here—Here, Now. For example, imagine that you have a goal of becoming a millionaire or a billionaire in a year. Think about this: why did you choose one year? It is a very arbitrary date or deadline. It is a mere grab at a date. It is possible that the Source can create that millionaire or billionaire outcome in an instant. Nothing is difficult for the Source, God. So why set a random date for the accomplishment of what can be accomplished in the blink of an eye, or at a time that is best suited for you that you may not have thought of right now?

Making deadlines for yourself also introduces fear and doubt and often actually slows you down. Will you make it by that date? What if you could have done it a lot sooner, but your mind kept looking at the faraway date? It also makes detachment difficult—and detachment is crucial for letting the infinite and unpredictable organizing power of the Source work optimally for you.

On the other hand, saying "one day I will be a millionaire or billionaire" is no good at all; in fact, it is even worse. Instead, think of Now as the only time. See it and know it to be the only real time. "I am Now a millionaire." Now. I Am. That is how you should always think, act, speak, and feel about everything. When people ask you when, say soon. Jesus always said "soon" when asked "when" by anyone. "Soon" fits a whole lot better in the Now-Here scheme of things than setting a specific date. In your mind, it's all Now, becoming, has always been.

Remember, even quantum physics proves to you that time is not what you think it is. When you say "I am a millionaire now" and the physical evidence around you does not show that, this does not mean that you are lying to yourself. Indeed, the moment of Now holds all existence in all possibilities, all at one time, including you being wealthy. That statement is true; it is your eyes that lie. Einstein once said that no matter how persistent the illusion of time may be—the illusion of past, present, and future—it is still an illusion.

—I am wealth. I am abundance. I am joy.—

Have patience with the unfolding of things. If you rush or force them, you interfere with them and slow them down. Nature is perfect. If you wish for faster results, the right way to shorten time is to raise your certainty. Increase the clarity of your imagination; be of one mind (do not keep changing your mind); concentrate; and, most important, raise your awareness from the level of your conscious mind only to that of your conscious, subconscious, and super-conscious mind and self. Most people are unaware of their subconscious and super-conscious selves. If you perfect awareness, imagination, faith, certainty, and clarity, you can create results instantly. You are now beginning, and you will get better as "time" goes by—just be deliberate in these things; choose to be more aware and certain, and it will happen. But do not be impatient, because that throws you into a state of wanting, and this delays results even further.

—I am wealth. I am abundance. I am joy.—

"I Am." Present tense. That is how your goals should be written. But it is useless to write them that way if you do not think about them in the "I Am," present-tense mode. Be aware of and deliberate in your thoughts and make sure that you always think of your goals and intentions in the "I Am" present-tense fashion all day long. "I Am" is a command to the universe to immediately get into the process of manifesting your wishes into physical reality. It is a declaration of the state of being in the moment of Now, Here.

—I am wealth. I am abundance. I am joy.—

You must understand and remember this very clearly, always. When you intend to have or experience something, you must know that you have it already. Really, you do have it already. All you will be doing from then on is receiving it, taking possession of it. Actually, you will be awakening to something that has always existed within you. Right now, as you read this sentence, you are already very, very wealthy. From now on, all you will be doing is taking possession of this wealth—receiving it or, more accurately, becoming awake to it. And be grateful now for the things you desire to experience, for you know you already have these things. Gratitude Now speeds up your experiencing what you choose, because it ascertains your faith and state of being.

—I am wealth. I am abundance. I am joy.—

Nothing is there to come, and nothing past. But an eternal Now does always last.

—Abraham Cowley

—I am wealth. I am abundance. I am joy.—

Time has only a relative existence.

—*Thomas Carlyle*

—I am wealth. I am abundance. I am joy.—

Time is a sort of river of passing events, and strong is its current; no sooner is a thing brought to sight than it is swept by and another takes its place, and this too will be swept away.

—*Marcus Aurelius*

—I am wealth. I am abundance. I am joy.—

When you sit with a nice girl for two hours, you think it's only a minute. But when you sit on a hot stove for a minute, you think it's two hours. That's relativity.

—*Albert Einstein*

—I am wealth. I am abundance. I am joy.—

There is a bridge between Time and Eternity; and this bridge is the Spirit of man. Neither day nor night cross that bridge, nor old age, nor death nor sorrow.

—*Upanishads*

—I am wealth. I am abundance. I am joy.—

Time is breath. Try to understand this.

—*George Gurdjieff*

—I am wealth. I am abundance. I am joy.—

Know the true value of time; snatch, seize, and enjoy every moment of it. No idleness, no laziness, no procrastination: never put off till tomorrow what you can do today.

—Philip, Lord Chesterfield

—I am wealth. I am abundance. I am joy.—

You wake up in the morning, and lo! Your purse is magically filled with twenty-four hours of the magic tissue of the universe of your life. No one can take it from you. No one receives either more or less than you receive. Waste your infinitely precious commodity as much as you will, and the supply will never be withheld from you. Moreover, you cannot draw on the future. Impossible to get into debt. You can only waste the passing moment. You cannot waste tomorrow. It is kept for you.

—Arnold Bennett

—I am wealth. I am abundance. I am joy.—

Eternity is the infinite existence of every moment of time. If we conceive time as a line, then this line will be crossed at every point by the lines of eternity. Every point of the line of time will be a line in eternity. The line of time will be a plane of eternity. Eternity has one dimension more than time.

—George Gurdjieff

—I am wealth. I am abundance. I am joy.—

What a folly to dread the thought of throwing away life
at once, and yet have no regard of throwing it away by
parcels and piecemeal.

—John Howe

—I am wealth. I am abundance. I am joy.—

The present is only a mathematical line which divides
that part of eternal duration which we call the future,
from that which we call the past.

—H. P. Blavatsky

—I am wealth. I am abundance. I am joy.—

According to Albert Einstein and others, time and space do
not exist as separate entities. Time is not a separate thing, and space
(made up of length, width, and height) is not another separate thing.
Rather, they are all one thing—called the space-time continuum. Try
to understand this and use it. Do not believe in time as something
separate from you that you have to go through as it dictates. If you
do not take time to understand time, it will rule your thinking, your
planning, your belief system, and your experiences.

Time is not a straight line that you have to walk. Imagine it to
be a network of tunnels under a city. To get from house A to house
B, you can use any one of very many routes, some longer and some
shorter. For example, in 1930, it may have taken thirty years of hard
work to make a person rich. Now it can take two years or less. We
have increased our wealth consciousness and certainty, and this lets
us take a shorter path.

Another way to think of the space-time continuum is as a sheet of paper that holds all possible events. Every event possible, everything, is on that paper. Now imagine yourself to be a pencil with an eye, and that this piece of paper wraps itself around the pencil. So you are the pencil and you are fully wrapped up in a paper that holds all events possible. But the pencil only has one eye, so you can only see the event happening on the piece of paper in the region where the eye is. The pencil's eye can travel up and down and around the pencil. It is a moveable eye that can go anywhere on the pencil's surface. The faster you move the eye, the more events you see. Now, imagine you can increase the size of the eye. The bigger you make it, the more events you see at the same time.

Okay, one last thing. Imagine you can multiply the number of eyes on the pencil. When the pencil has more eyes, it sees more "life"—more events simultaneously, instead of one at a time. When you increase the number of eyes and size of each eye, you see more in less "time." Okay, replace the word "eye" in this whole explanation with the word "consciousness." An increase in the size and number of eyes is an increase in consciousness, in being "awake" to all that exists. That is what our evolution as beings is all about—increasing consciousness. Okay, so what is the pencil? Your Self—your spirit, or soul, whatever you wish to call it. You are a timeless and multi-dimensional being, made in the image and likeness of the Source, God. And as you grow, you increase your consciousness and awareness of this fact.

Now, imagine that your best friend is another pencil with the same piece of paper wrapped around him or her. You are both pencils with eyes, with the same piece of paper wrapping around you. When your "eyes meet," you experience the same bit of All That Is at the same time. You decide to meet by choosing to meet. You can choose to meet anything you wish in that continuum; there are no blocks, and free will works without error if you exercise it with certainty. Knowing this is *power*. Using this knowledge for wealth and any other desire you have in your life is *joy*.

This is how you can explain all interaction. In truth, you and your friend and everyone else are just individuations of the same pencil, so when your "eyes" (consciousness) meet, you experience being together, but you are always together on a higher level.

—I am wealth. I am abundance. I am joy.—

Events that appear simultaneous to you may occur at different times for another observer, depending on his or her relative motion. Imagine you are in a big box on a truck moving from south to north. At the center of the box is a light bulb that goes on and off periodically. The light strikes the north wall of your box at the same time that it strikes the south wall. You can even measure this and find it to be so. You will find that it strikes all walls simultaneously. This will be your truth.

Now suppose that there is a woman at the side of the road, and that your box has a glass window. The woman can see inside your box through this window. Because she is stationary and you and your box and bulb are in motion, her experience will be different. She will see that the north wall is getting light slightly after the south wall because the north wall is moving away from the light while the south wall is moving toward it (remember that the truck is moving south to north and the bulb is in the center of the box). She can even measure this to be so. She finds that the south wall gets light earlier and the north wall later. This will be her truth. Thus, two contradicting yet accurate truths can coexist. How is that?

To the universe, these are just events. Time is local to the observer, to you. In reality, there is no time, only all events all at once. It is your motion through these events that makes you feel as if there is time. It is your expansion of consciousness that makes you move faster through more events. An expanded consciousness enables you to take in more events per moment. An increase in wealth consciousness makes you get rich faster, move through more events faster, see more events more quickly. In reality, it brings you into the awareness and experience of more of All That Is per moment, so that you appear to have more "stuff," and so appear to have more wealth.

It is also the increased number of right choices you make and the increase in the desires and goals you make with certainty that make you experience more at any moment of Now. By increasing your goals, your mental images, and holding them steady and certain, you "see" more wealth. That is one of the secrets of time.

—I am wealth. I am abundance. I am joy.—

Hermann Minkowski, Einstein's mathematics teacher, came up with a set of equations that prove that the entire past and future of an individual person all meet at a single point—Now—and in a single place—Here (wherever the individual is doing the observations).

—I am wealth. I am abundance. I am joy.—

All events in the universe are all occurring simultaneously at this eternal moment of Now. The illusion we have of them occurring one at a time, in a sequence that seems to flow, results from the type of awareness or consciousness that we have in our human form. This causes us to see very narrow sections of the space-time continuum at a time. So we see one small slice, then the next, then the next, and so on. But we can expand or contract our slices to take in a lot more or a lot less. A person of wealth consciousness has a highly expanded view of All That Is, thus a much-expanded experience.

—I am wealth. I am abundance. I am joy.—

Everything which for each of us constitutes the past, the present, and the future is given in block ... Each observer, as his time passes, discovers, so to speak, new slices of space-time which appear to him as successive aspects of the material world, though in reality the ensemble of events constituting space-time exists prior to his knowledge of them.

—*Louis de Broglie, Nobel Prize winner*

—I am wealth. I am abundance. I am joy.—

Time only exists in your mind. Your mind often wants to live in anticipation of the future or in memory of the past. This is also what creates psychological time to a large extent. This is another "time." There are many forms of illusionary time, and psychological time is one of them. You experience this type of time when your mind is anticipating something in the "future" or remembering something in the "past." This "anticipating" and "remembering" creates time, as well as a lot of pain and stress. It is unnecessary. The most fruitful thing to do is not to remember or wait; it is to observe, experience, and create—Now. Observing, experiencing, and creating Now is timeless; it is the true nature of the universe.

Everything happens Now. You remember your past Now. You dream your future Now. You learn from your past Now. When you were actually in your past, it was still Now. At that point in the past, if someone were to ask you what you were doing now, it would still be Now. You work toward your future Now. You will get to your future Now. You will live in your future Now. You are always Here, Now. You cannot Be anywhere else. Being, Is-ness, is only Now. There is nothing you can do in any other moment except Now. Try it. Do something yesterday or tomorrow right now. Impossible! You can only Be and Do Now. It is all Now. Even "tomorrow" is happening Now, is

Now. You see how eternity works? It is inescapable. And trying to escape Now in your mind is futile and painful. It is like trying to not Be where it all Is. That is why the Buddha, Jesus, and many other masters taught us not to worry about the future. They taught us to be still, to be present, to be aware, to enjoy Now, to live one moment at a time, and to be conscious.

An easy way to see how time is largely a creation of the mind remembering the past and anticipating future is to consider your experience when you sleep. When you go to sleep, you can "clock" eight hours of sleep; yet when you wake up, it feels as if you spent no time at all. It feels as if you just went to sleep a moment ago. You do not feel as if you have gone through eight hours in the same way that you do during the day when you are awake. Yet, as you know from research reports, people dream pretty much throughout the night, although they remember just a few dreams—if any. See, it is the no-mind, the no-memory, and no-future escapism that makes you feel as if sleep is almost timeless. When you sleep, your mind and your soul are at the same place, together. And that place is Now, always.

—I am wealth. I am abundance. I am joy.—

All other things held constant, to the extent that an individual or society is aware of, teaches about, and uses the illusion of time in the right way, so will it have wealth and happiness.

Time is directly related to consciousness, and consciousness is what makes you experience your life. There is a clear and direct link. You now know this, so you are much more aware. This awareness will start leading to your increased consciousness. This increase will lead to more wealth. You may not notice it at first, but as long as you stay committed to your intention to be wealth-conscious and aware, it will happen. You may not know exactly when it will start happening. In truth, it already has. You will just see that, as days pass, you are becoming more awake with each passing moment, until one day, you look back and see how much you have really changed.

Do not worry if you have not fully understood the illusion of time. Read on and the coming chapters will make things clear. There will always be more to know—the layers never stop. But as you peel each new layer and discover deeper truths, you will enjoy life and turn it into a thrilling ride. But always stay balanced.

Now that we have the four dimensions covered and we know what our experience here on earth is constructed of, we can now take a look at what constructs it. Who does the construction? What causes this construction? First, we'll look at how states of being, thoughts, words, actions, and the laws of the universe all contribute to the building of the universe, and how space and time influence that construction.

Then we'll have a look at the builder. Who is this builder? You are. All beings are builders and co-builders. So the question is really: How would you build a happy and very wealthy life?

CHAPTER 4

Images of the Mind:
The Blueprints of Life

THE NEXT STEP TO GETTING WEALTHY is to know how life works. In other words, how does the force of life take instructions and turn them into things and new moments out of the quantum energy field? What type of instructions does life take so that it may create each new moment in your day? What is the format? What are the specifications?

This chapter will answer these questions for you. They are the most basic questions, but they must be answered before we get progressively deeper into the essence of wealth. In fact, you may have heard the principles in this chapter before; they aren't really new. Yet few people understand them fully and even fewer use them, despite their simplicity.

Imagination is a very basic, but integral, part of becoming wealthy. Every other part of the process uses the imagination at some stage. Your mind's images are literally the blueprint from which your world is built.

In the chapter on quantum physics, you saw scientifically how physical reality is produced. In the following chapters, you will see imagination's interconnections with life. But first, let's look at imagination, both as the images of the mind, and in and of itself.

Life is images of the mind expressed. What this means is that life, the Source, uses your thoughts, your mental images, as the instructions by which to create your reality in the material world. Life expresses your mental images into physical reality. To express is to make known, to state, to articulate, to communicate, to convey. The force of life makes known your thoughts to yourself and everyone else by forming them into experiences and objects that can be recognized here in the physical world. You experience your own thoughts firsthand, your images of your mind, so that you may know which ones are suitable and which ones are not. That is how you know yourself; that is how you experience your Self; that is how you grow. This is the supreme purpose of this physical world that we are now in. It is designed to enable you to experience your Self. It is designed to enable you to experience an idea and its effects and consequences.

Life does not select which of your images to express and which ones not to. How would it choose for you? It therefore expresses all of them to the extent that you have them and believe them. You have true free will. This free will is truly free because it acts without filtering or favoring. Free will is truly free because it actually gets results all the time, not just some of the time, and it gets them exactly. Later, we will see exactly how free will works, even when it looks as if it were impossible for it to do so.

—I am wealth. I am abundance. I am joy.—

Imagination is the force that takes you to places you have never been. Napoleon Hill said that imagination is the most marvelous, miraculous, inconceivably powerful force the world has ever known. Life is imagination, images of the mind, expressed into physical form. Feed your imagination daily and accurately with pictures, movies, and concentration. Spend time doing this in detail every day. Imagination is the most powerful force because life uses it to know what to create next. Most people spend little time imagining. They imagine using idle thought in a haphazard way and wonder why their lives are not rich for them. Imagination has the power to make or break your life. It is your mind, and your choice.

—I am wealth. I am abundance. I am joy.—

Images. Images. Images! Life is images of the mind expressed. Imagine your life as you wish it to be—picture perfect, with color and details, in your mind, every day. Spend an hour a day doing your images. And throughout the rest of the day, keep your thoughts in harmony with your images of your chosen life. This is so important that it cannot be overemphasized. The Source, God, works perfectly, giving you exactly what you envision and think about. Exactly. No more, no less. It is therefore extremely important that you have crystal-clear images and thoughts, consistently.

For example, many people wish to have a nice car. But the mistake they make is to have "get a nice car" as their goal. What do they expect the universe to give them? There is physically no such car called "nice car." Be crystal clear! Envision the exact car you desire— its make, model, color, and options. Go to the car dealer or look it up on the Internet and know exactly, or as exactly as possible, what it is you wish to have as a "nice car." Then envision that every day—the more you think about it, the closer you get it to you. This is the effective way to image.

Life is images of the mind expressed. Do you wish to travel to another country for a dream holiday? Go to the travel agency and get all the details—brochures, flight itinerary, prices, hotels, and car reservations. Build up the whole trip, exactly, in your mind in full color and spectacle.

–I am wealth. I am abundance. I am joy.–

Life is an expression of inner images. Everything we do and experience is an expression of our images, our imagination, and our thoughts. Work on your images. To change your life, change your imagination and change your thoughts.

–I am wealth. I am abundance. I am joy.–

The life that you are living is the life that you have imagined.

–I am wealth. I am abundance. I am joy.–

Envision and imagine every aspect of your life as you would like it to be. Do this daily for at least an hour. Your life is images of your mind, expressed to the extent that they are believed.

–I am wealth. I am abundance. I am joy.–

Walt Disney, against all odds, criticism, and a string of "failures," stuck to his imagination and became the entertainment king of the world. Mickey Mouse was created at the lowest point of his "failures." No one could have predicted that an empire would be launched by a mouse. When we willingly go where our most desired imaginings take us, we become creative forces that have no limits. Albert Einstein said that imagination is the greatest creative force. Learn to be willing to go where your imagination and desire take you.

–I am wealth. I am abundance. I am joy.–

If you wish to give your visualization a boost, use the eight hours of sleep you have each day. It is easy to learn how to be "awake" in your dreams. In such a state, you can be an author of your own dreams, painting your perfect life and living in it during your dreamtime. Remember that the subconscious mind cannot distinguish between real and imagined experiences. And dreams can be the best form of visualization. This skill is called lucid dreaming, and there are several books that can teach you this skill.

—I am wealth. I am abundance. I am joy.—

Have many reasons to live and be wealthy. The more reasons you have, the more wealth you will get into. Instead of having paid bills as your only reason to get wealthy, have reasons like travel, collecting art, buying homes, having beautiful clothes, expressing your love to others with gifts, treating your friends and family to some good things, buying a boat, saving the environment, and so on. Visualize these reasons accurately. Reasons convince the subconscious mind, the heart, to internalize the goal. They also give it working substance. The more reasons you have, the more powerful your imagination will be and the faster you will get your results.

—I am wealth. I am abundance. I am joy.—

Surround yourself with images of things you like. Get brochures and magazines of vehicles, homes, places, things, bodies, sports, and activities that you like. The clearer your images of your visions, the clearer and faster you will achieve them.

—I am wealth. I am abundance. I am joy.—

Dream big and hold the dream high enough—and consistently enough—and the dream must manifest into form, by law. By universal law, it cannot fail to do so. Do not worry about how. It is all taken care of for you as long as you do your part by thinking, acting, speaking, and being in accordance with that dream. Just dream and visualize, and then start doing something. Do the next thing that you feel you should do in accordance with your dream, and keep on moving. The little that you do will trigger something else you did not foresee—and on and on it goes until your dream is a reality.

—I am wealth. I am abundance. I am joy.—

Are you dedicating at least thirty minutes of your day exclusively to visualizing and imagining your future? Life is images of the mind expressed. Imagination is what designs your life. Have dedicated imagination time, but also hold those visions high in your mind all day long.

—I am wealth. I am abundance. I am joy.—

The world is an illusion, as we will see much more clearly as we move on. See it as an illusion; believe it to be an illusion, an illusion designed to help you know and experience your Self. Once you do so, you will always remember to create the next version of the illusion that you wish to have. You literally create the next version of the world by painting your mind's images with certainty. The world does not have to be as it is; it simply is because we all agree it is.

—I am wealth. I am abundance. I am joy.—

Your subconscious mind cannot tell the difference between a clear and vividly imagined experience and a real experience.

—I am wealth. I am abundance. I am joy.—

Visualization creates a new subconscious. Visualize your wildest dreams and fantasies. Live large! Back it up with faith, belief, and certainty.

—I am wealth. I am abundance. I am joy.—

The subconscious mind is where your self-image is stored. It powers your conscious thoughts and your actions. Reprogram it using visualization and belief, and you reprogram your world. Your world is your self-image revealed to you in a way that you can experience it.

—I am wealth. I am abundance. I am joy.—

Your life is your images, your imaginings expressed into physical things. More accurately, it is the manifestation into the physical world of the visions, good and bad, that you believe in most—consciously and unconsciously.

—I am wealth. I am abundance. I am joy.—

How to do the impossible? Let your imagination fly.

—I am wealth. I am abundance. I am joy.—

Get excited about your images. Energize them with positive emotion. Emotions are energy in motion. Gratitude is one of the most powerful of these emotions. Infuse every cell of your body with your images. Infuse every cell with the gratitude that you have realized your goal already, even if you are not experiencing it now. You have received it automatically by the perfect laws of the universe (even before you ask, it has been given to you). And when you act, remember to infuse this same gratitude into your actions.

—I am wealth. I am abundance. I am joy.—

You chose the images. The Source, God, does the work effortlessly and perfectly. That is the deal.

—I am wealth. I am abundance. I am joy.—

The conscious mind creates impressions in the subconscious. It does so by repetition. The subconscious mind then expresses these images, or causes an expression of them, into physical manifestation. The conscious mind does not cause expression. It can only impress on the subconscious mind using repetition and faith, belief, certainty. The reason this is so is that the conscious mind holds all sorts of thoughts—those you believe in and those that you do not. It is like a wild monkey, jumping on very many thoughts throughout the day. The subconscious mind, on the other hand, holds only what you hold as truth to you, what you believe in. It holds your sponsoring thoughts. That is why only the subconscious, or what some call the heart, causes expression.

—I am wealth. I am abundance. I am joy.—

Your subconscious mind only takes in the affirmative and not the negative. If you visualize and set the goal "I am not poor anymore," it will only take in "poor." Instead, change that to something like "I am rich, wealthy, and abundant." The subconscious mind does not internalize "not"—it does not internalize negations. It only internalizes "I Am" something, not "I Am not" something.

—I am wealth. I am abundance. I am joy.—

Repetition is power. Concentration is power as well.

—I am wealth. I am abundance. I am joy.—

When visualizing your goals, see yourself already in possession of what you desire. Say and think "I Am," not "I will be." This is critical. "I Am" is power. Later, you will see how this is scientifically so. Now is the only existing moment; all others are illusions.

—I am wealth. I am abundance. I am joy.—

All other things held constant, to the extent that an individual or society has positive and grand images in the right way, so will it have wealth and happiness.

Now that you have the basics of creation covered, let us move on to progressively larger things. Carry with you what you now know about images, for you will need it to keep building your understanding of wealth. The larger lessons that follow will enable you to understand this lesson on images more deeply—experientially, scientifically, and spiritually. Let's keep moving on.

CHAPTER 5

Thinking and Speaking:
The Instructions of and for Life

C LOSELY RELATED TO IMAGES ARE THOUGHTS. Just as life is images of the mind expressed, it is also thoughts of the mind expressed. In other words, life is the mind expressed. Your external reality is the densest part of your mind, without any separation. The separation between you and your outside world is illusory. As we move on in this book, you will come to see firsthand how this is so—scientifically and spiritually.

Life is your mind expressed. The outer world is the densest part of your Self; it is an extension of your mind. When you finally stop believing in the illusion of separation, your power will rise dramatically. But even now, you can still change your mind to change your world. You will now see how this happens and, as we move on further into this book, you will see further scientific evidence of this. Eventually, the illusion of separation will fall away totally, and you will have mastered this truth. But even now, just knowing this is empowering.

This chapter is a course in how to think in ways that are friendly to the universe and its laws—ways that co-create the universe itself purposefully into one that you wish to live in and not one that you just find yourself in. In this chapter, we'll talk about the laws of the universe in a way that will help all the pieces of the puzzle fall into place.

Okay, let us dive into the mind. Your world is the densest part of your mind.

Life is your thoughts expressed. To paraphrase what we learned about images, life, the Source, uses your thoughts as instructions for creating your reality in the material world. Life expresses your thoughts into physical reality. To express is to make known, to state, to articulate, to communicate, to convey. The force of life makes known your thoughts to yourself and everyone else by forming them into experiences and objects that can be experienced here in the physical world. You experience your own thoughts firsthand, your images of your mind, so that you may know which ones are suitable and which ones are not. That is how you know yourself, that is how you experience your Self, and that is how you grow. This world is designed to enable you to experience your Self. It is designed to enable you to experience an idea and its effects and consequences.

—I am wealth. I am abundance. I am joy.—

Your state of wealth externally is an extension and testament of your state of wealth internally. How clear and certain you are in thoughts of wealth is evidenced externally.

—I am wealth. I am abundance. I am joy.—

Life does not select which thoughts to express and which ones not to. How would it choose for you? It therefore expresses all of them to the extent that you have them and believe them. You have true free will. The will is truly free because it acts without filtering or favoring. Free will is truly free because it actually gets results all the time, not just some of the time, and it gets them exactly.

—I am wealth. I am abundance. I am joy.—

To the extent that your thoughts are not conscious, deliberate, and focused in any topic of life, you will be affected by the outcome of the thoughts of other people. And to the extent that your thoughts are clear, focused, and noncontradictory, your results will be sped up. A few people are able to perform what many people call miracles simply by thinking strongly and in a focused way about only one thing. The idea that the outcome of their intention may not happen as they wish it to happen does not even occur to them for a split moment.

—I am wealth. I am abundance. I am joy.—

Suffering is always the result of an error in thinking. It is an indication of being out of harmony with the laws of the universe. The only purpose behind the existence of suffering is to show you when a thought is in error and alert you to the existence of a higher thought that would serve you better. Suffering stops as soon as that higher way is found, that higher thought. In the presence of suffering, try not to resist. Instead, examine with an open mind, and the answer will always show itself to you without fail.

—I am wealth. I am abundance. I am joy.—

Concentration gives thoughts more power and speed in achieving goals.

—I am wealth. I am abundance. I am joy.—

Your dreams, thoughts, and visions will build your world. You will rise and fall with the rising and falling of your thoughts.

—I am wealth. I am abundance. I am joy.—

Repetition breeds integration and internalization. To attain wisdom, read this material repeatedly and think in the right way over and over again. Through repetition, things are embedded into your subconscious. They cross over and become you.

—I am wealth. I am abundance. I am joy.—

You can predict the future by looking at the thoughts, words, and actions of today and applying the law of cause and effect to them.

—I am wealth. I am abundance. I am joy.—

You are never denied answers to your questions. Whatever questions you ask earnestly and with conviction will be answered exactly. No more and no less. If you earnestly and with conviction seek and ask how to earn one million dollars, the universe will conspire to bring you the knowledge, tools, people, and events to give you that answer. If you ask how to earn a billion dollars, you will also get answers worthy of that amount. Einstein was not born a genius in mathematics and physics. He simply asked the right questions, earnestly and with conviction. You see, the universe works by a perfect law that never once errs or favors particular people. Once you understand that the universe's deep, complex, yet simple rules are perfectly balanced, you cannot fail to succeed. Whenever you see chaos and unpredictability in the universe, you are simply seeing something that you do not yet understand. But it is nonetheless something that is organized and predictable by certain laws. Nothing is difficult for the Source, God. And perfection and balance is the nature of the Source. Hence, all laws are applied equally, universally, and unfailingly. Just ask the right questions earnestly and with conviction.

—I am wealth. I am abundance. I am joy.—

Be specific and do not keep changing your mind. All thoughts count and produce results. Changing your mind all the time "confuses" the universe. Imagine walking into a travel agency and saying,

"I wish to travel." Then you look at the agent blankly. He or she is ready to make your reservation, but cannot until you say where you wish to go. Imagine you now say: "Well, I'd like to go to Moscow and Timbuktu at the same time." Again, the agent cannot fulfill that request. Now imagine you say: "OK, then book me to Moscow. No, wait, Timbuktu. No, wait, Moscow. No, wait; I am not sure I can afford it. No, I can. No, maybe I don't wish to go there or travel at all." This is how many people think all day. And the universe is "confused" by their thoughts, just like the travel agent. This indecision produces "confused" results for them.

—I am wealth. I am abundance. I am joy.—

Whatever you put your attention to gets energy from you and grows. Remove the attention and it dies. Be conscious and deliberate in this. Intention goes along with attention. What you intend and give attention to begins to become.

—I am wealth. I am abundance. I am joy.—

We become what we think about. We are the sum total of our thoughts.

—I am wealth. I am abundance. I am joy.—

All laws of nature always work; they can never fail even once, for that would cause chaos in the universe. The nature of the Source is perfection. You become what you think about, without fail. If you think about wealth, without any contradictory thoughts, you will become wealthy, without fail.

—I am wealth. I am abundance. I am joy.—

Matter is merely materialized thought.

—I am wealth. I am abundance. I am joy.—

Always be calm. A calm mind is unaffected by fear-causing and anxiety-causing situations. Never proceed in a confused and anxious state of mind—the thoughts you have in that state are erratic and suicidal. Calm down first and remind yourself of the laws of the universe before you proceed.

—I am wealth. I am abundance. I am joy.—

Thoughts attract like thoughts. Souls attract like souls. Minds attract like minds. It is a reciprocating dance. That is how it works. It is also correct to say that thoughts attract like matter, and matter is objectified thought—that is, thoughts made into objects. Also, the body and the world is a denser extension of the mind, and the mind a subtler extension of the body and the world. They are not separate. Use this knowledge to understand and recreate your surroundings, your wealth, and your health.

—I am wealth. I am abundance. I am joy.—

Do not let your mind dwell on dissatisfaction even if you are now feeling dissatisfied. That only feeds and supports dissatisfying conditions. Change your attitude; look at these conditions as perfect outcomes of your past thought and as an opportunity to recreate yourself anew. Thank them for this gift.

—I am wealth. I am abundance. I am joy.—

The combination of intention, belief, and detachment enables you to move through life calmly, knowing that the universe always fulfills your intentions, but does so in the most appropriate fashion using sequencing and intelligence beyond your comprehension. Life starts working out and you start smiling, marveling at how all things seem to just work out for you. When you face a challenge or a problem, you can relax, because you know that it is all part of your intended outcome. It will all be solved for you. Even before a challenge or problem comes up, it is already solved. It is only there to take you one step closer to your desired and intended outcome. With this approach to life, you will find life working out automatically for you, based on the desires and intentions that you back up with belief. As you practice this and get more confident and relaxed with this new way of living, old habits of fear, anxiety, frustration, and "failure" will fall off gradually, and you will start succeeding faster and faster. And as you get better at it and become more aware and conscious of your whole Self, the time between thought and its physical manifestation will shrink. Ultimately, it can disappear altogether. Indeed, there have been and are people who have this ability.

—I am wealth. I am abundance. I am joy.—

The most amazing thing about life, as many have discovered, is that the act of creation is very much an act of realizing that something was already there. The universe is designed that way. It is all Here, Now—all that could possibly be. We are able to experience what is already there through choice, and that choice is made increasingly possible by increases in our understanding and perception of life.

—I am wealth. I am abundance. I am joy.—

Have intentions, but not preferences or addictions. Choose future outcomes by your intentions and desires, but accept all present moments. Present moments are the perfect outcome of your past thoughts, states, and actions. They are a gift to you to enable you to experience yourself and grow. Resisting and cursing the present only perpetuates its nature.

—I am wealth. I am abundance. I am joy.—

Speak to yourself and ask yourself your questions, expecting an answer. You will soon develop a knack of getting answers from within. They come as feelings, not words; but you can get what they mean, you can get the gist or the *gestalt* of them.

—I am wealth. I am abundance. I am joy.—

Learn to distinguish between genuine feelings and thoughts or emotions that mask themselves as feelings.

—I am wealth. I am abundance. I am joy.—

When you intend something, be of one mind. Don't equivocate between options or hesitate over preferences. Practice detachment in the moment of Now. Accept joyfully what is happening in the present, for you have brought it with your previous thoughts, words, actions, and state of being; and it is only here to let you have a look at yourself, like a giant living mirror. What you resist persists. Do not wish your present were different. Live happily in your present. Be of present mind, but make choices about your future and intend your future with one, single mind, clear focus, and precision.

—I am wealth. I am abundance. I am joy.—

Never stop learning.

—I am wealth. I am abundance. I am joy.—

Observe and affirm the truth, and the truth will set you free. If you are broke, say so. Look it in the eye. Admit it. Then look to see the errors in your thinking that caused it. Always affirm the truth, for what you resist persists; what you face and bring into the light releases you. But be careful in how you admit your error. Don't just say: "I am broke." It is more correct to say: "I previously had thoughts, actions, and states of being that led to this manifestation of being broke that I am now observing." In fact, never say, think, or feel negative thoughts. "I am" statements are always carried out by the universe.

—I am wealth. I am abundance. I am joy.—

Change the cause, not the effect. Thought is cause. Physical reality is effect. Trying to change the effect directly is like banging your head against the wall. For example, if your sales have dropped, it may not be because your marketing is wrong. It could be that you have a negative attitude to your business or an aspect of it. People have attitudes like: "I hate going to work"; "I hate this job"; "I hate this customer-service task"; "I wish I could just relax and do nothing all day." If you have them and you are wondering why no matter what you do in your business things are not working out well, this could be a cause. Dig deep, be aware, and analyze your state and thoughts. They are always at the root cause.

—I am wealth. I am abundance. I am joy.—

Now here is something that may take some time to ring true. Understanding this brings enormous power. Remember how we saw that you are the cause of things that happen in your world? Those who have taken time to study and experience this know experientially that every person causes 100 percent of their world. Now, remember that thought takes time to manifest into the physical, depending on the subject matter. So what are you looking at when you use your eyes to see things? What are your eyes seeing? If you are the cause of all you see and thought takes you time to manifest, you are obviously looking at yourself at various stages of your "past." Read that through again.

It is all an illusion—an illusion designed to allow you to look at yourself so that you can create the next version of yourself. You can design your growth. What you see with your eyes is an illusion

designed from various stages of your past. The real you—your Self—
is very far ahead. Your thoughts right now are extremely close to the
real you, dragging behind just a fraction. The real you is that which
causes the thought—the wordless you from which thought springs,
the observer, the soul. But that's another topic. Let us get back to illusions and how to use them to create wealth. The way to use this world
you see with your eyes is to see it as your past and actively and deliberately use it to observe your Self and see what to change and how to
grow. That is one way to use the illusion, which is a gift brought to you
kindly so that you may know your Self.

—I am wealth. I am abundance. I am joy.—

Present results are the effects of previous thoughts. In other
words, when you look at the world today, you are actually looking
at yourself as you were yesterday. The world at any present moment
of Now reflects your thoughts and states of being before the present
moment of Now. It is all an illusion. Use it as the illusion that it is,
and you will live wonderfully and richly.

—I am wealth. I am abundance. I am joy.—

Insanity is doing the same thing repeatedly and expecting a different result. What are you doing? Are you doing the same thing every day and expecting a different result? If so, have a good laugh now,
a hearty laugh; then change from this moment forward—from Now.

—I am wealth. I am abundance. I am joy.—

There is such a thing as a sponsoring thought—a thought behind a thought. And a sponsoring thought has more creative force
than a sponsored thought. What we normally call thought is actually sponsored thought. Look at your thoughts closely. They have a
sponsor, a cause. If you think you need to eat food, that thought has

a cause behind it, a sponsoring thought—in this case, the belief that you are hungry. Start becoming aware of these sponsoring thoughts. They come from your subconscious mind, or what some people call the heart. Sponsoring thought reflects what you truly believe in and hold true. It is your subconscious programming. If your thought and sponsoring thought over something are uncoordinated, if they do not agree, the sponsoring thought wins. That is why people who pray to God begging for something never get their prayers "answered"—because their sponsoring thoughts express "not having" or "lacking." Be aware of and correct your sponsoring thoughts.

—I am wealth. I am abundance. I am joy.—

Science has proven that deep meditation temporarily shuts down the part of the brain that tells you where you "end." Meditate, and you will reach a vastness of mind and consciousness that you never thought possible. Business solutions, new business ideas, and wealth strategies are just a fraction of what will begin to arise. It has been said that, if you do not go within, you go without.

—I am wealth. I am abundance. I am joy.—

Judge not, condemn not. These thoughts cause negativity and maintain that which you judge or condemn. They cause retardation and a whole host of nonproductive results.

—I am wealth. I am abundance. I am joy.—

Expanded perception causes expanding wealth. Forgiveness causes the expansion of your perception. When you forgive others and yourself for what you think has been done wrong, you become open to seeing what you and others truly are. You become open to seeing the beauty and capability that you may have missed. You become more tolerant, and you embrace freedom and love. You start to believe less in conditionality. Many things happen that expand your perception. And expanded perception expands your consciousness, your abilities, your opportunities, your contacts, and a lot more that leads to wealth.

—I am wealth. I am abundance. I am joy.—

You become what you think about earnestly and with conviction most of the time.

—I am wealth. I am abundance. I am joy.—

By some accounts, you think about 50,000 thoughts a day. Some are thoughts that make you walk and scratch or control your physiology. Others are unconscious daydreams. Many are repetitive. But only a few of them are conscious and deliberate. Start watching your thoughts, being aware of them. Do not let them remain random as they may have been. Make more and more of them conscious and deliberate. By becoming aware of your thoughts, you will wake up and become a deliberate designer of your life. You become aware by simply deciding to be aware.

—I am wealth. I am abundance. I am joy.—

Turn your mind into a sunny beautiful island that allows in only positive thoughts and influences, and absolutely shuts out every negative thought or influence. Act as if you have an alert positive-mind defense force in your head that is on twenty-four-hour active duty defending you against internal and external negativity. And it has to win all encounters.

—I am wealth. I am abundance. I am joy.—

Form a mastermind group. This is a group of people of like mind. Get together frequently and exchange ideas, materials, and motivation. Where two or more are gathered, the power multiplies, and the power of the whole is more than the sum of the power of the parts. A mastermind group is very powerful. It multiplies the power of each participant greatly.

—I am wealth. I am abundance. I am joy.—

When a negative thought comes up, at that instant say "Stop!" Immediately move on to a positive thought. Do not even entertain the negative thought for a second. But remember that this is different from resistance to negative thoughts. What you resist persists. There is a big difference. Negative influences can come up from friends, TV, news, your imagination, things you see, and so on. When you notice these negative influences and thoughts arising, shut them down instantly. There should be no resistance involved. If you find that the negativity is so strong that you feel you have to resist it—that you cannot simply go around it without using resistance—then face the negativity head-on. Do not resist it. Instead, bring it into your light, face it, and examine it with detachment. Try to look at it directly from a detached point of view to see what it is composed of, why it is arising, and why it is affecting you in that way. Break it down and understand it; understand what powers it. Ask yourself why it is there, what it really is. By being mindful and watching the negativity, studying its composition and finding its root causes and answers, you are able to overcome it.

—I am wealth. I am abundance. I am joy.—

You get there in your mind first. We climbed Mount Everest in our minds first. We got to the moon in our minds first. You learned to walk in your mind first. Get where you want to go in your mind first. It's that simple. Anything you wish to have, have it in your mind first. If you wish to have a massive new house, have it in your mind first in exactness and detail. Live in it in your mind first, and it will follow in physical form.

—I am wealth. I am abundance. I am joy.—

Try to avoid reading or watching bad news as much as possible, even if you think it is good for your business. Bad news creates bad images that interfere with your grandest vision. The world appears to you as you choose to see it. Bad news is often a self-fulfilling prophecy.

—I am wealth. I am abundance. I am joy.—

Now, you know that thoughts create your reality. But if you are trying to link all of your reality today with your thoughts today, you are making a mistake. Today's thoughts affect some things today, but some of the more "solid" things in your reality today are the result of many days of past thoughts. Depending on their subject matter, focus, and certainty, thoughts take varying amounts of "time" to manifest into physical form.

—I am wealth. I am abundance. I am joy.—

Think about your thinking. Think about the things you think about. Watch your thoughts and be deliberate in them.

—I am wealth. I am abundance. I am joy.—

Thoughts are timeless and forever. You can intend and create into the past just as effectively as you normally intend into the future. Most people never consider this possibility, yet it is a powerful and useful one. This ability lies in the timeless nature of spirit and in the timeless nature of the quantum energy packets that are the building blocks of the entire universe.

—I am wealth. I am abundance. I am joy.—

What has become physical can be changed by thought, but it is a lot harder to change what is already physical than it is to make physical what is not already in physical form.

—I am wealth. I am abundance. I am joy.—

What does it mean to pray ceaselessly? Consider this. It has been said that even before you ask it is given unto you. It has also been said that if you ask, it shall be given unto you. Do you catch that? Asking is not begging. You do not beg the Source, for it is already given to you even before you ask. Begging and wanting simply give you a lack of that for which you beg and yearn. This is not just a spiritual idea; it is also provable using quantum physics.

The quantum "soup" literally contains all possibilities of everything, Now, Here. In other words, that spiritual promise is also a scientific fact. It is also said that you can do anything if you believe. And it has been said that whatever you put your attention and intention to takes form. That is how you create things out of the quantum "soup" of pure energy—by attention, intention, and belief. Many masters, teachers, and sages from all cultures and times have told us not to worry, to practice detachment, to trust in the mysterious workings of the universe—not only because the universe works with supreme intelligence, but also because you may not be aware of what your soul or higher self is choosing.

Here, then, is what it means to pray ceaselessly. You have a desire; you will it to come into being, to manifest. You intend it wholeheartedly, clearly, in a focused way, and with certainty. You pass this intent on to the Source, in whatever way you know how. Simple intention is enough, although meditation—stillness—is more effective when you have the time.

So you pass on your intent, and you become detached from it. In other words, you watch it from behind the scenes, without a desire that it should happen in any particular way or "time" or sequence. And because you know this works—because of your certainty and consistency, your detachment and gratitude—your intention will take form in the most unexpected and miraculous way. That is prayer.

Praying without ceasing is going through the whole day, every day, with focused intention for all your life's desires, with certainty, detachment, and gratitude. You don't do this just once at a special time during the day and then act totally differently and remained confused the rest of the day. Praying ceaselessly has to become a lifestyle. That is, prayer is meant to be active, ever-present, and part of your normal wakefulness. It is co-creative with the Source; it wills to action; it is self-assertive. It is not the periodic, passive, helpless, and emotional appeal that many of us were taught to conduct as children. Ask and it shall be given unto you; seek and you shall find. Yet before you ask, it is given unto you. Be self-assertive, co-creative, ever-present, and grateful. Intend to receive and don't beg—that is praying without ceasing. Get rid of the idea that prayer is the same as begging God for a favor. Lose your sense that God chooses whether or not to grant this favor and comes down and does both your work and his own.

Prayer is actually will, and will is co-creative. Your part of it is to use clear intention, certainty, gratitude, detachment. You must have certainty; you must know you have this power; and you must trust that the Source is friendly to your plans. To the extent that you do so, your prayers, your will, will be "answered." There is no criterion by which the Source decides to grant or not to grant prayers. The laws of the universe apply to all equally and unfailingly. Prayer is an inward energetic process, a call you give out with a detached expectation of an answer, without a shred of doubt. It is strong and certain will. When you realize that even the request is unnecessary—that you are one with All That Is, including whatever it is that you wish to have, and that you are the granter and conveyer of that wish—you will truly be praying and receiving without fail. For your prayers will be of pure gratitude for what is already given unto you, even before you ask. The request is not necessary. Just be grateful and smile!

—I am wealth. I am abundance. I am joy.—

Play ceaselessly, as well. Have fun with life! Life is joy. The essence of life is joy. Where there is joy, creation is abundant. It is easier to create wealth where there is joy, and joy gives meaning to wealth.

—I am wealth. I am abundance. I am joy.—

What you think in your mind and feel in your heart is what you become.

—I am wealth. I am abundance. I am joy.—

Everything you see around you was someone's idea. Look around you. Nothing can exist before it first exists as an idea in some mind.

—I am wealth. I am abundance. I am joy.—

As a man thinketh, so shall he become.

—The Bible, Proverbs 23:7

—I am wealth. I am abundance. I am joy.—

Your mind is infinite.

—I am wealth. I am abundance. I am joy.—

All other things held constant, to the extent that an individual or society has positive and grand thoughts in the right way, so will it have wealth and happiness.

Well, yet another building block is covered. You now know how to think and speak in the right way for wealth creation. We have one more step to cover in the thought field. We saw how images work. Images are an aspect of thought. Then we moved up to cover the whole of thought itself. And now we shall cover the last aspect of thought—goals.

CHAPTER 6

Goals: The Road Map to and in Wealth

THERE IS A CERTAIN WAY in which you should set your goals. What are goals really supposed to do? Goals get you thinking in the right way to wealth. Goals focus your thoughts, format them in the right way for the universe, and keep your images consistent and non-random. Hence, there is a right way to set goals.

A lot has been said before about the importance of setting goals. This is nothing new. What you are about to now see, however, is quite likely new to you. You will now see how you should set goals to get to wealth fast. Setting goals is all well and good; but setting goals correctly is tremendously powerful.

Welcome to the world of powerful goals! Your goals are a prophecy of what you shall one day become.

If you do not know where you are going, you will end up exactly there (where?). If you fail to plan, you plan to fail. If you have no specific goals, you will get no specific results. Remember, the Source takes your thoughts, your mind's images, and manifests them into your reality. You saw exactly how this happens scientifically in the chapter on quantum physics. But your thoughts and images are the blueprint by which your world is designed and created by and for you. Goals are planned thoughts, directed thoughts. Without planned and directed thought, your life will be unplanned and undirected, seemingly haphazard and seemingly unreliable.

—I am wealth. I am abundance. I am joy.—

Simply know where you are going, and the answers as to how you will get there will come to you in their own time. Do not worry about it. Simply believe that you will get there.

—I am wealth. I am abundance. I am joy.—

Your ideas, visions, and dreams—whatever they may be—are the prophecies of what you shall one day become and achieve. You can predict your outer life tomorrow by looking at your inner self today. You can change your tomorrow by changing your inner self today.

—I am wealth. I am abundance. I am joy.—

Take goals seriously. A twenty-year study involving students in a certain Ivy League university in the United States traced the lives of one graduating class. Three percent of that class had their own written goals at the start of the study. By the end of the twenty years, that 3 percent was worth more financially than the other 97 percent combined. They also reported more satisfaction and joy in their lives.

—I am wealth. I am abundance. I am joy.—

The visionaries and dreamers of the world are the saviors and driving force behind it—the inventors, artists, philosophers, educators, sages, business people, designers, scientists, leaders, and anyone who dreams big and creates. The world lives in their ideas and ways, and it cannot let their ideas die fruitlessly. The world is beautiful because of the dreamers and visionaries. The world and the universe as a whole are in full support of these dreams, if only the dreamers will believe this and act that way. The universe, the world, the Source, God, is friendly and supportive of your dreams and aspirations. Simply have a vision, believe in that vision, and you will without fail realize it to the extent that you believe you will. All else is in your favor. So dream very big! Dream very, very big indeed!

—I am wealth. I am abundance. I am joy.—

Conformity can be your worst enemy. If you do what the crowd does, you will get what the crowd gets. Every day, people get up in the morning, go to work like everyone else, and do things like everyone else. But ask them why they do it, and they'll tell you that they really don't know. They just work hard all day because everyone else does, and their reason for working is that they wish to pay their bills and provide for themselves and their family.

If you are thirty years old and working hard like everyone else, like the rest of the crowd, and that is all you are doing, you can easily tell, roughly, where you will be in life when you turn fifty by looking at the fifty-year-old crowd today. Are most fifty-year-olds today financially independent or wealthy? No, they are not. The vast majority of people today are not wealthy or financially independent. But they could be, if only they chose not to follow the crowd just because "that's the way it's done."

To get something better than the crowd gets, you have to do one thing different. You have to have specific goals, reasons, visions, and wealth consciousness. By reading this book, you have started on your way to something different and wealth-causing. By practicing what you read here daily, you complete the requirements for wealth.

Realistically speaking, you can be self-made, wealthy, and financially independent even at eighteen years of age or less. It all depends on how early, strongly, accurately, and certainly you start your goal-setting, your visioning, and your wealth-consciousness building. Hard work alone is not the key to wealth. People have gotten wealthy with and without hard work. Wealth consciousness as a whole is the key. And goal-setting in the right way can provide the map.

—I am wealth. I am abundance. I am joy.—

There is a common mistake people make when they achieve their goals—a mistake that takes them back down. The best way to understand this mistake is to illustrate it. Let us say that a person has a goal of having a million dollars in their bank account soon, and now they have $4,000 in their account. So they do all the right things—set their goals, visualize, get certain, act, and do all that. They keep their vision of that million high, and they achieve it. Now when that account shows one million dollars, they get happy, of course, then they make the mistake. They start looking at the bank account, trying to maintain their precious old goal, worrying when it drops below their goal level, and so on. They switch their sights from that of an unachieved higher goal, and they start looking at the achieved past goal. They start living in the past, trying to maintain the past. Then they start worrying, and it goes on like that until they lose that million dollars. They stop doing what they were doing right in the first place to get to their goal, and they start living as they used to.

Always set your goals higher than your present reality. This does not mean that you are never going to be satisfied with your achievement. It doesn't mean that you should get greedy. No. On the contrary, it means that you should enjoy every day without worry. You should not worry about losing what you have. You should not worry about maintaining that million you just made. Instead, make the million, and enjoy making it and having it. But when you reach that million, do not switch to worrying about keeping it. Instead, set a new higher goal and keep your eye on that new goal while you enjoy your old successes without worrying about maintaining them. In any case, it is folly to worry, as the worry itself is what will bring you down.

Wealth consciousness and all its activities are a lifestyle, not something you do occasionally. Your thoughts, being, and goals should always be on the next grander version of you, not the past version.

—I am wealth. I am abundance. I am joy.—

Be careful how you set your goals and visions. The heart, also called the subconscious, has a tendency to take in and internalize the un-negated part of a vision or statement. For example, if one of your goals is never to miss paying your bills on time again, it can be harmful to make the goal statement: "I will never miss paying my bills again." In fact, only the "miss paying my bills again" may be taken in because that statement brings up fear as soon as you say it. Instead, make the statement: "There is always more than enough money to live the life I choose, to enjoy myself, and to invest."

—I am wealth. I am abundance. I am joy.—

Failing to plan is planning to fail. Plan and set goals and visualize them. Master this skill.

—I am wealth. I am abundance. I am joy.—

Always keep your goals beyond your comfort zone. If you achieve all your goals and fail to create new bigger ones, you stop growing. That can be dangerous, even though it may feel comfortable. Did you know that most people start getting the symptoms and diseases associated with old age within a few months of retirement? Through retirement, they signal to their brains and body that life is now wrapping up, coming to an end, and that society does not require their services any longer, so certain functions can now start to switch off. Retirement is not the problem; it is the signals that people accept that is the problem. Again, there is nothing wrong with retirement, but watch your signals. The lack of goals can be dangerous to your health, unless it is what you wish to have. Goals do not have to be about money and career. There are countless worthy things to set as goals that have nothing to do with making money or a career—personal goals like sports, travel, and hobbies, as well as global goals like environmental and charity work.

—I am wealth. I am abundance. I am joy.—

You do not ever have to know how you will reach your goals. Just do your part, let go, and you will reach them.

—I am wealth. I am abundance. I am joy.—

Do not live by accident or by default. Live by design. Design your life using goals, visualization, imagination, and plans—all done consistently, daily, clearly, accurately, and with details.

—I am wealth. I am abundance. I am joy.—

It is not enough to set goals. Goals must be set in a certain way, a right way that is most friendly to the universal laws. Here are the right steps for setting goal:

1. List what you would like to have, to do, and to be between now and the next thirty years. List everything you can think of, small and large—places to visit, things to have, residences, experiences, partners, skills to acquire, things to do, people to meet, projects, charities, health, habits—everything! This is not a list of what you think you can achieve. It is a list of what would give you the most incredible life whether you think you can achieve it or not, a life that would be unbelievably fantastic for you. Your list should have at least 100 things on it; it is

not hard to come up with 100 wishes for thirty years. If you wish to be very wealthy, have about 5,000 things—even small details regarding your desires should be in there.

2. For each goal you list, write the reasons why you wish to have it. If, for example, you wish to have a large home, write down the reasons why. In other words, what will you do with and in this home? Put drama into it. Reasons empower your goal and make it easier to imagine, visualize, and attain. They give life to it and make your subconscious accept it more easily.

3. Get cuttings from magazines, brochures, the Internet, photographs, etc, of the items in your goals and stick them in your journal. Start a Goals and Visualizations Journal on paper or your computer. In it, place pictures of the things you wish to have—cars, stocks, buildings, boats, land, travel, clothes, or anything else. Refer to it often—twice a day is highly recommended. The more real and detailed your visualizations and imaginings, the faster and more accurately you will realize your goals. Pictures are very important to have in your life.

4. Every day, read your list and look at your pictures. Then spend at least twenty minutes twice a day imagining, animating, and visualizing in detail all your goals. If you meditate—and it is highly recommended that you do—do your goals visualization in meditation as well. Meditation puts you closest to the Source, the best place you can be to plant your seed of visions into the field of infinite possibilities and creation.

5. Then, Here, Now, do something that takes you closer to your goal. There is always something to do now, however small, that will open the next step to you—a step that may be unseen until that first step is taken. Every act is an act of self-definition

and creation. Act deliberately and with awareness so that each act takes you closer to your goals, not further from them. Act with purpose.

6. Do everything with gratitude. Think, speak, and act with gratitude—the gratitude of knowing you are guaranteed success if you act in the ways of these laws. Gratitude is a statement of certainty. That is power. Be genuinely grateful and excited about the fact that you already have your goals realized, for they are guaranteed by universal law. This type of gratitude works wonders.

7. Enjoy the fruits of your efforts; enjoy experiencing your goals when they manifest into your reality! They are sure to do so, guaranteed by universal law.

—I am wealth. I am abundance. I am joy.—

Make sure your Goals and Visualization Journal is portable. No point writing a journal that only stays home. You should also record important thoughts in it that you have, as well as experiences and conditions. Record as much as possible in your journal—at the end of each day or whenever it is most convenient for you. A journal greatly helps you discover and create yourself accurately. Do not worry about the structure of your journal; just make it easy to use for you.

—I am wealth. I am abundance. I am joy.—

In your journal, also write problems you encounter. Suffering is an error in thinking, as you will see later in the chapter on conditions. Writing down your suffering helps you evaluate it clearly and discover your errors.

Write down your feelings as well. This is very important because true feelings are communications from the soul, that part of you that is closest to the Source. Do not confuse feelings with emotions and thoughts; be careful about that.

Write down good ideas and inspiration as soon as you get them. Perhaps the best time to get inspiration in a waking state is when you first wake up in the morning. Instead of immediately taking on the baggage and planning of your day, stay in bed and ask and think about some big idea that you want to know about, and it will come to you very clearly. When you wake up, before you are fully awake, relax and gently ask yourself the most important questions of your life, gently without arousing yourself. The answers will come to you in amazing ways, in ways that they never do during the rest of the day. Once you start practicing what is in this book, ideas will start coming to you in large numbers from all sorts of sources, seemingly by coincidence.

Have your journal handy. Do not wait to write later; write now, before you forget or "lose it." And do not forget to record the dreams that you have at night; one day you will find them useful—all in good time. Dreams are not just useless images that come to you as you sleep. People think of the time they are awake in the day as their "live" time; they think of sleep as their "rest" time. They think that all their decisions and useful actions are accomplished when they are awake. Well, the amazing thing is that you—your Self, soul, or spirit, however you wish to refer to it—never sleeps. Your spirit or soul or whatever other term you are comfortable with never ever sleeps. It just changes states of consciousness, dimensions of consciousness.

You are multi-dimensional. Waking is one state or dimension; sleep and dreams are another. And there are many more. And they all count; they all influence your life in the waking state. And vice versa. Even if you do not believe this, remember that all thoughts count; and dreams are thoughts, so they count and, of course, influence events in your life. You never really sleep, so to speak. You are a soul with a body, not a body with a soul. To the extent that you are conscious of this and awake to it, so shall you have more of All.

—I am wealth. I am abundance. I am joy.—

To make it easier to refer to your journal later, you can do the following:

- Have separate parts of your journal for different types of information.

- Make an index at the back.

- Use different colored pens.

- Stick tabs on pages you wish to mark.

Or you can invent any other system you like that ensures easy access to your information.

—I am wealth. I am abundance. I am joy.—

Review and reread your journal at least once a month, preferably more often. Once a year, read all your journals. When you reread, you start seeing your life in a completely new light all at once. You see successes you never thought you achieved; you see things you should change; and you see errors to correct. The whole point of keeping a journal is to review it. It can open up amazing opportunities to understand yourself better, to see more clearly, and to grow faster.

—I am wealth. I am abundance. I am joy.—

In making entries in your journal, enter the exact date, time, and location. This helps you track down patterns, trends, and rates.

—I am wealth. I am abundance. I am joy.—

The more events and experiences you capture in your journal every day, the more you will get out of it.

—I am wealth. I am abundance. I am joy.—

Get into the habit of carrying your journal with you.

—I am wealth. I am abundance. I am joy.—

When writing down and speaking of your goals, write in present tense, "I Am…"

—I am wealth. I am abundance. I am joy.—

"I Am…" "I Am…" No matter what you are trying to create next in your life, find a way of putting it into an "I Am" statement. For example, if you wish to lose weight, do not think or say "I will lose ten pounds," or "I want to lose ten pounds." Instead, say, think, and write "I am X pounds now." Do the same with wealth. The only time that exists in the universe, scientifically and spiritually, is Now. Hence "I Am."

—I am wealth. I am abundance. I am joy.—

Do not worry how your goals will be fulfilled. There are powerful forces at work in all of nature, with infinite intelligence and coordination. Things, people, books, places, TV shows, movies, etc, will start appearing and helping you achieve your goals. In other words, "coincidences" will happen. Simply visualize your goals with conviction.

—I am wealth. I am abundance. I am joy.—

Shut out all other thoughts that negate your goals.

—I am wealth. I am abundance. I am joy.—

The trick is in the details and in consistency. For example, if having a new home is a goal you have, write it down in detail. Write down where the house is located, how many rooms it has, the size of the compound, the size of the home, the furnishings in it, and so on. Then visualize it that way. And do not change your mind—this is very important. Understand that the universe is actively manifesting into physical form all your thoughts. Every single one of them turns into some amount of physical form somehow and somewhere. If you change your mind, you will be undoing your own work. Just hold your thought until it becomes fully physical.

—I am wealth. I am abundance. I am joy.—

Target dates for goals are best set to the eternal moment of Now. Even if you are setting up a goal that you would like fulfilled ten years from today, state it and think of it in the present tense. Setting an arbitrary date in the future introduces a state of wanting and waiting. Wanting prevents achievement. Arbitrary target dates also interfere with the natural functioning rate of the universe, which you do not usually know. When you say, "By the end of next year I will be a millionaire," how do you know that you could not have become one by the end of next month? Anyway, the only real time and place there is in the universe is Now, Here.

—I am wealth. I am abundance. I am joy.—

Be exact. Define your goals and visions exactly.

—I am wealth. I am abundance. I am joy.—

If you aim at nothing, be sure you will get nothing specific. Talent, intelligence, and hard work without exact goals often lead to frustration.

—I am wealth. I am abundance. I am joy.—

A Happy Pocket Full of Money

Thoughts take time to manifest into physical reality. Most people only think a few months ahead. Today, they may think: "I need to buy a house soon." Then they start stressing over it and struggling to get it. That is the haphazard, short-term approach. Try a long-term approach. Imagine the power of setting goals thirty years in advance. By listing and visualizing daily everything you would ever like to have over the next thirty years, you set in motion the forces and power of thought and the universe well in advance. Even if you do not wish to buy a house now, as long as you know that one day you will or may wish to buy one, start visualizing it now. Thoughts take "time" to manifest into physical reality, so the earlier you start, the better. Life then starts working automatically. You start realizing your goals in time without stress and time pressure. Things simply fall into place. Remember in your thirty years of goal-setting that, even though you think you need something twenty-five years from now, you should set and think of that goal in present tense, Now. "I Am" and not "I will have." The universe will take care of the appropriate timing for you.

—I am wealth. I am abundance. I am joy.—

You have to know where you wish to go if you wish to make sure that you get there. Otherwise, you will not get there. Have goals, plans, images, and visions. Have journals to record, track, and refine them. Without goals, plans, images, and visions, you will not go very far—or at least not as far as you are capable of going.

—I am wealth. I am abundance. I am joy.—

How many goals should you have? You can never have too many. The wealthiest people have hundreds. Some have thousands. Some have so many goals that it would take 200 or 300 years to manifest them all. You should aim at having at least 5,000 goals. To understand why, you have to understand the nature of goals.

- Goals are images of the mind, the stuff that the universe uses to create. So the more you have, the more you give the universe to work with, and nothing is impossible or difficult for the Source.

- Goals have a tendency to "just come true" at the most unexpected times and in the most surprising sequence. The more goals you have, the richer your life experience will be.

- When you reach a goal, its power disappears. You no longer have a driving force, and the universe no longer has anything to work with. So the more goals you have, the better.

A person with one goal will achieve less than one with 100 goals. A person with 100 goals will achieve less than one with 1,000 goals. The fewer goals you have, the less you will achieve. The more you set, the more you get.

How can you possibly have 5,000 goals? Easy. Think of details and of everything connected with your desires. List everything, even small things like "have lilies in my garden," "decorate my grandmother's house for her, "stay at the Ritz," "donate to the Wildlife Conservation Fund," "buy a BMW convertible, a Jeep, a jet, a boat," "have a salt-water aquarium in my living room," "get my father a golf set," "buy books for orphaned children," "take a trip to the Great Wall of China," "meet these people," "date these types," "work with these groups," "buy this type of shoes," "wear clothing from this designer," "have this type of chairs from this shop," "wear these ski boots," "see these places in these countries," and so on. You can never run out of things that you would love to do, be, and see on this planet!

The more you have these wishes in your awareness, the more you will start meeting with "coincidences" in your life that make them come true. Life starts working magic, and you have passion and excitement. Remember, wealth is abundance expressed. Again, wealth is abundance expressed, translated into physical form, manifested. Abundance is all there is; it is your true nature and the nature of life. When you think of wealth, do not think only of money and business. Think of everything, everything that you wish to have, do, be, or see in your life and the lives of other beings—all life.

Here is the greatest insight: you are merely an observer. Life gives unto life all on its own. In any case, it all exists. All you do is observe and experience. Try to understand this. You are an observer with a body to experience your observations. It is what you choose to observe and experience that determines what you observe and experience. It is all there for you, automatically. So choose many things, and you will see many things.

Another thing you should understand about goals and thoughts is this: Your goals are caused by you and everyone else, and vice versa. In other words, when you intend to have a boat, it causes an inspiration in a person suited to build boats to get into the boat business. It also inspires all the necessary events and middlemen to take part appropriately to bring about your having that boat. Everybody wins. What do you think caused this book to be written for you? It is the effect of your previous desire to be wealthier, the desire of billions of other people to be wealthy, and my desire to spread wealth and be wealth. It is because you desire that a thing is created—without your desire *nothing* is created, and *all* you desire is created. You can correctly say that you wrote this book.

Life gives unto life; you are an observer with a body to experience your observations. That is how it works. You observe what you choose to observe. You experience what and how you choose to experience. The more goals you have, the more you allow life to work through you for the good of all. Life's ultimate goal is to express itself, and it does so effortlessly, following your exact intentions and beliefs.

Once you see this clearly, you will know without a shred of doubt that what you wish to have wishes to be with you more than you wish to be with it. Life wishes for nothing more than to express itself. So do not be shy now; have many, many goals!

—I am wealth. I am abundance. I am joy.—

Do not make the mistake of formulating your goals only in terms of money. Wealth is abundance expressed. Abundance means plenty of everything. Money is only a small aspect of wealth. Many people "fail" to get wealthy because they plan their goals in terms of money only. They say something like "make enough money to buy that car" or "make a million dollars to buy a house." There is a huge error in that sort of goal-setting. Another mistake is to have huge financial goals and very few other goals. Some people may set goals like "make a billion dollars," but they have few other goals. Why are both of these errors? Try to understand this clearly: life is images of the mind expressed. It is that simple. Life is also precise. You automatically get exactly the amount of money needed to realize the most precise and certain images of your mind. And although you may think that money is the only way to get a certain thing that you would like, life knows that there are many other ways of getting it, not just through purchase with cash. So if you have very few other goals and images in your mind, if you hardly think of anything else except money, there will not be much "material" for life to work with.

To illustrate, imagine that it were possible to open up a person's mind for examination. Now imagine that there are two fictitious people—John and Mary—and they both wish to be wealthy. Mary wishes to have a billion dollars, and that is all she thinks about. On examination, her mind shows few images of anything else. There are even very few images or goals related to her business or job—to customer numbers, quality, products, and so on. There are also few images and goals on all other aspects of her life. Mary has just one strong wish, desire, and goal—to become a billionaire.

Now John also wishes to be wealthy, but, unlike Mary, he also has cultivated many interests and desires in all aspects of his life. His mind, on examination, is full of vibrant images of a wide variety of many other things. It even has specifics on small details like the clothes he wishes to have, places to travel to, the decor in his offices, ways he wishes his customers treated, gifts he wishes to give to his loved ones and the rest of the world, and so on. Now the question is, all other things held constant, who do you think will become wealthier and in a much easier and seemingly coincidental and lucky way? John, of course, will be the wealthier and in an easier way.

Life ensures that all of your mind's images that you hold true and clear are fulfilled. It is okay to wish to be a billionaire, but how exactly do you visualize a billion dollars! You see, the lack of lifestyle visualization is why many people "fail" to achieve their financial goals. It is very hard to visualize and hold fast in your mind a billion dollars. But it is extremely easy to visualize the lifestyle and business of a billionaire!

Do not separate your financial life and goals from the rest of your life, for the financial goals are only a means to an end, not an end in themselves. Remember, money is a shadow of value, a medium of exchange. Your goals should be on the value and the exchanges, not on the money, the shadow.

—I am wealth. I am abundance. I am joy.—

Be of a state of mind that allows the Source, life, God, only to say yes to you, never no. The only question, then, is this: What is it that you are asking for, and do you believe in it? Don't ask for something; intend it. For even before you ask, it has been given to you. Whatever you ask for, whatever you intend earnestly and with conviction, shall be yours.

—I am wealth. I am abundance. I am joy.—

Without vision we perish.

—The Bible, Proverbs 29:18

—I am wealth. I am abundance. I am joy.—

A major reason why people lose wealth is that their goals diminish and their images fade. Sometimes this happens when something new comes into your life, and you forget the original passion that made you wealthy in the first place. This new thing may be the birth of a child, the finding of a love partner, the achievement of comfort—especially if you come from a poor background and then get rich. None of these things are "bad," but it is good to know and keep in mind that, if you ever find yourself "going down," reexamine your goals and mental images. That is a powerful start to your finding out what is happening in your life, for life is images of the mind expressed.

—I am wealth. I am abundance. I am joy.—

Read many magazines on all topics. Magazines give you ideas, images, goals, desires, and much more. The more images you have in your mind, the richer your life will be.

—I am wealth. I am abundance. I am joy.—

All other things held constant, to the extent that an individual or society has positive and grand goals in the right way, so will it have wealth and happiness.

This wraps up our journey into thinking in the right way for wealth. Images, thoughts, and goals need to be created and focused in a certain way. Then they must be fitted into the bigger picture. In reality, thinking is the second step in the wealth-creation process, but it is often the most involved and active step in creating wealth. Never, ever forget, however, that thinking is only the second step of wealth creation. It is very important that you always remember this.

So what is the first step? It is Being, First Cause. It is that which causes thought. That from which thought springs. That without which thought would not be. Let us dive in deeper still.

CHAPTER 7

Being: First Cause—
The Beginning

B EING IS A STATE, LIKE BEING HAPPY. You cannot explain a
state, nor can you *do* a state. You can only be a state. You cannot
do happiness; you can only be in happiness or be happy. Creation works like this: being causes thinking, which causes speaking,
which causes doing, which puts in place the system to receive and
experience what you created in your being and thinking. Being is the
First Cause. Let's break this down step by step.

Being causes thinking. So when you are happy, you will think
happy thoughts. Thoughts spring from being. In other words,
thoughts are sponsored by being. In fact, nothing happens without
being. As you will see in later chapters, even conditions occur because
of a state of being, and not the other way around, as most people
think. Happy conditions do not make you happy. Being happy causes
happy conditions. Unhappy conditions only show up to demonstrate
your preexisting state of unhappiness. By the time you finish reading
the chapters on cause and effect and on conditionality, you will see
clearly how this is so.

The first step to experiencing massive wealth is being wealthy. Being wealthy is an internal state. It has nothing to do with the outside world. The internal state of wealth is a decision you make right now and you become it, right Now. You need nothing outside of yourself to make this decision. Once you make this decision to be wealthy, you become wealthy. It is hard to speak of this, because you can only *be* a state (you cannot *do* a state or *speak* a state). We shall now try to speak *of* this state and, when you finish this chapter, you will see clearly how being works and how you can be wealthy right now.

Be wealth, Now, Here, just like that.

Be wealth. Do not try to get wealth. Be wealth. To help you understand this, consider happiness. Do not try to get happiness, be happy. See? You can either try to do things that make you happy; or you can instantly decide to be happy. Just make a decision. You have done this before at other times in your life. Everyone has at one time or another said: "You know what? I am not going to let this bother me. I am going to be happy and stop worrying about this." Which is easier? Trying to do things to be something, or being that something instantly and letting that state of being allow you to do things consistent with it? Of course it is easier to be happy than trying to get happy. And this is the same with wealth. Be Wealth. And everything else will follow automatically, as long as you are always, at all moments, Being Wealth. Just Be It.

—I am wealth. I am abundance. I am joy.—

As you will see throughout this book, and as you saw in the chapter on quantum physics, all that can possibly exist exists in the eternal moment of Now, Here. Even the version of you that is wealthy and experiencing wealth already exists. If you are not experiencing wealth right now, you are just not conscious of it or awake to it. When you choose to be in a certain state right now, here, you activate the fastest forces of creation. Then you immediately move your consciousness to that other you (in this case, the wealthy you). Being is the fastest way to create things, because it causes an instant shift. Material manifestation follows instantly to the degree that you have become a state without doubt. Again, to the degree that you have become a state without doubt, your reality will quickly shift to reflect it. As impossible as this may sound now, it will all make sense when you consider the real workings of this universe, especially after reading the quantum physics and conditionality chapters.

—I am wealth. I am abundance. I am joy.—

The fastest way to create is simply to be, right now, whatever you wish to create. Then do not negate it by thought. Do not think about it. Just be. All your thoughts, words, and actions after that should be of the new state you chose to be. If you are not wealthy and you wish to become wealthy, just decide right now to be wealthy from this moment on—from Now. Do not think about it; just choose to be it. From then on, all your thoughts, words, and actions should be of yourself as a wealthy person. In Ultimate Reality, this is not a lie to you. You are actually all things anyway, even though you may be experiencing small sections of the All. By choosing to be something else, you cause your environment and circumstances to shift to experience the new state.

—I am wealth. I am abundance. I am joy.—

Remember, thought comes from being. A state of being is what causes thought. A state of hunger causes thoughts of hunger. Being is the First Cause. Being is; thought is doing. Being just is. Being takes no time; but thought takes time to bring things into being. So the fastest way to wealth is being wealthy, now, instantly. Change your being to a wealthy one. Do so by deciding right now and knowing it to be so with certainty, against any "evidence" to the contrary in your physical world (which is an illusion anyway). Do it with certainty and clarity and keep holding that state of being. Know you are wealthy, for in Ultimate Reality, you really are actually very wealthy indeed. And you will very quickly begin to experience this wealth, very quickly indeed. Not many can pull this off, because they doubt it is true; but we all have the capability to do this. Simply declare, knowingly and certainly, "I Am . . ." And then don't think about it again; that will only introduce delay and doubt. Here is an example. Remember the last time you were in a state of being broke or sad? You did not consciously think about the state, questioning whether it was real, whether you were really broke or sad. You just took it for granted that you were; you believed it unquestioningly. You just were that state, and that was that. You were simply it. Now try taking wealth for granted. Be wealth, believe it, and make it so—no questions asked. The universe will obey.

—I am wealth. I am abundance. I am joy.—

The sequence of creation is as follows:

- The unified field of consciousness that is non-physical (God, the Source) individuates itself into non-physical units (individuated spirits or souls of various beings and objects).

- These units take on individuated physical forms—the objects, people, and beings that we see.

Whatever you see physically is created in this sequence from, of, and by the Source of All That Is, God. You are a co-creator in this creation sequence; you create together with the Source, in the same sequence.

In regard to wealth, therefore, you can now see how futile it is to look at your individuated physical aspects (your bank account, your material wealth, your body, etc.) and let what you see influence your individuated non-physical aspects (your mind and thoughts and state of being). That is tantamount to looking at the results and letting them influence the cause. It is like short-circuiting the system. It will only lead to enhancing of your current physical state. For example, if you look around you and see that you are broke, and you let that dictate to you that you are a "broke" being, and you keep thinking from a "broke" point of reference, and you think "broke" thoughts and thoughts of inability, you will remain broke.

The key is never to look at the ground, never look at the physical and let that dictate to you that this is who you are. You are not your conditions; you simply cause them. The correct thing to do if you are broke is simply to choose your greatest vision of yourself—a vision of wealth—and keep that state of being—those thoughts of wealth—steady and ever-present. Act as if you are wealthy, no matter what your physical world looks like, no matter how impoverished your physical world may seem. This will turn around the physical to match your thoughts and state of being. Always remember, the physical follows the spiritual and the mental. It is the design of the universe.

—I am wealth. I am abundance. I am joy.—

One way of creating things in this world is by thoughts, words, and action. But this is the slow way to go about it. The faster way is by a change of state. Being. For example, when you say that you are hungry, that is a state. When you are confident, that is a state. You are be-ing. You need nothing outside of yourself to be in a certain state. To acquire wealth, it is much more effective to be in a state of wealth, to make your being one of wealth, to feel wealthy and to think, speak, and act wealthy. You will have a hard time becoming wealthy if you feel poor and then think, speak, and act wealthy. Your state—how you feel about yourself, your being, your "I Am" declarations—is the fastest way to acquire wealth. The way you change your state is to decide to change your state. Simple. And you can do it now. It is like being unhappy and simply deciding that you are tired of being unhappy. So you just decide to be happy. Everyone has done this before. Now do it with wealth.

—I am wealth. I am abundance. I am joy.—

Expect to experience massive success! Always maintain that state of knowing that you have and experience abundance. Expectations like these, knowing at this level, cause attraction and remove repulsion. This is extremely important. Expect massive success. Know yourself to be powerful.

—I am wealth. I am abundance. I am joy.—

You can remember the past and look toward the future, but you can only be yourself Here, Now. Your be-ing can only be Here, Now. Being, manifestation, is only Here and Now. Millions of people consume their waking hours with their minds trapped in daydreams, worries, and other non-present-moment thoughts. They are awake but very unaware of their full surroundings Here, Now. Wake up! Smell the coffee! This simple waking up will produce an amazing change in your life. Try it, commit to waking up, one day at a time. This, combined with "I Am" present-tense thought and visualization, is an amazing speed boost for achieving your desires.

—I am wealth. I am abundance. I am joy.—

What you are so is your world. Everything in the universe is resolved into your own inward experience. It matters little what is without, for it is all a reflection of your own state of consciousness. It matters everything what you are within, for everything without will be mirrored and colored accordingly.

—James Allen

—I am wealth. I am abundance. I am joy.—

To get wealthy outside, get wealthy inside using the information in books like this one. To become a billionaire, raise your images and certainty to equivalent levels and act with certainty, with your purpose infusing your actions. The world is inside you. Nothing and no one slows you down or speeds you up except yourself. To the extent that you recognize this, you will change your world. Wealth is a whole lot easier to acquire than you may believe. It is simple. The hardest part of wealth acquisition is the taming of your own mind, a thing that is totally within your own control.

—I am wealth. I am abundance. I am joy.—

It is correctly said that success is something you attract by the person you become.

—I am wealth. I am abundance. I am joy.—

What is being? You cannot think being, you cannot act being, you cannot talk being, you can only experience being. Being is Isness; it just is. Being is consciousness. Being is of no mind. In fact, sometimes mind can destroy being what you wish to be. Being is something you choose to be, right Now. Not later, but Now. When you start thinking about it, you destroy it. Once you are, you are. Any thought after that should not be about whether or not you are; it should only be to fulfill that state of being, to experience it rather than determine it. It is often a good idea to be of no mind. Be still.

—I am wealth. I am abundance. I am joy.—

Thinking has its place. It is a tool, just like your arms and legs. You do not use your legs all the time. You only use them when necessary. Your mind is a powerful tool. It makes many things possible. Yet it is so powerful that it often takes you over. Your mind should only be used when necessary. And it is only necessary about 10 percent of the time. Research has shown that about 90 percent of our thoughts are repetitive. Most of them are worries about the future or memories of the past. This is clearly unnecessary. The only real moment is Now. Trying to escape Now is the cause of much tension and "failure" and trouble in our world. Your normal state throughout the day should be one of no mind. You should be a watcher, not a thinker. You should watch your mind. Just as you observe the things outside of you, start observing your thoughts as well. In this way, you cease to be under the control of your mind. You stop identifying with your mind and identify with your Self, the all-knowing being. You start living in the present instead of reliving the past or anticipating the imaginary future. Your tensions fall away and your success blossoms.

However, do not judge your mind or curse it if you realize you have been under its control. It is a beautiful tool if only you can learn how to use it correctly. You already know how to use it. Use it only to make your intentions, to give life its appropriate images to bring forth new experiences into the moment of Now, and to work with things in your moment of Now (not five minutes from now, but right Now). You will start to notice that, in the moment of Now, you never have any problems—you have events, but not problems. Problems exist in your mind, in your thoughts. As events, they are just things that happen and change as soon as they happen. In fact, mind is the cause of many of the events Now and of their sustenance. All your problems, if you have any, are imaginary and in the "future." If you are still alive reading this book, you know that you have never failed to get through the moment of Now. If you are here reading this, then you never failed a moment of Now; you never failed to get through Now successfully. Even death, the ultimate fear for many people, is not a problem. Those who know what death really is also know that it is not a problem; hence, they do not fear it. Nothing in Now is a problem.

Nothing Now is a problem; you are designed to execute Now perfectly. But the minute you start worrying about the future, identifying with your mind instead of using it, you start having problems. Remember, the future does not exist. It is in your mind. Even when you think of the future, you think of it Now. When you actually get to it, you get to it Now, not then. At the time you actually *are* in your future, it will still be Now.

Be the observer of your thoughts. You are not your mind. Your mind is a powerful and beautiful tool, but never identify with it. Use it to think in the right way, and turn it off when you are not using it. In truth, you do not need to use it most of the time. Think about this. Have you ever been in a life-threatening situation that just popped right up in your face unexpectedly? What happened then?

Your mind may have done some things, but it mostly shut off. Your Self, Being, took over and, in a most intelligent way, handled the situation in the best way possible. In any true emergency, when the mind has no time to think about things, you usually become present in Now and it is never a problem when you do become present. In fact, you become extremely calm. Now here is the good news. You do not need an emergency to access this calm, super-intelligence. You can learn to be there all the time, to be present all the time. That is true Being. Being is no mind. Being is Is-ness, presence, awareness, consciousness, Now.

—I am wealth. I am abundance. I am joy.—

Your thoughts, words, and deeds reflect your awareness, your consciousness, your being. Change your being, and you change your world. You can change your being in two ways. One way is simply to choose, Now, to be what you wish to be, and hold that intention. Another way is to act as if you were what you choose to be. Act as that state. Then speak as if you are that state. Then think as if you are that state. Sooner or later, your being will follow suit.

—I am wealth. I am abundance. I am joy.—

The words "I am" are potent words. Be careful what you hitch them to. The thing that you are claiming has a way of reaching back and claiming you.

—A. L. Kitselman

—I am wealth. I am abundance. I am joy.—

All other things held constant, to the extent that an individual or society has positive and grand states of being in the right way, so will it have wealth and happiness.

Think about what you have just read about being. It is a lot to take in, but it is easy to do it; it is simple. As long as you are willing to do so—like a child who is willing to learn new things of the world and to believe in them—you will find it easy to understand being and to change your being. To the extent that you are willing to be like a child, to simplify and do things just because, you will be able to understand and internalize this chapter.

Do not worry about what some of the teachings you just read mean. Some of the meanings, the real meanings, will only become clear after you have read the whole of this book. They are explainable using other concepts. The chapters on conditionality, self, one, cause and effect, time, and quantum physics will especially deepen your understanding of being and how it literally works. For now, however, let us get into the next stage in creation.

Being is the first step, First Cause. Then follows thinking, then speaking and writing (words), then acting. Speak as you think. We will not have a chapter here on speaking because words are simply thoughts expressed. Simply look at what has been said about thinking and apply it to speaking. Just because we do not have a separate chapter here on words, however, does not mean that they are not important. Words are very important; they are thoughts expressed, and they have a tremendous impact on creation.

We shall now turn to acting—the right way to act to receive the gifts of wealth.

CHAPTER 8

Acting: That Which Receives

ONCE HAD A DREAM that I was sitting on a small stool about six inches high, and this old and very friendly but vigorous man was sitting on a bigger stool, teaching me some lessons. And he said: "You cannot run this world by actions. You can only run it by the Word." And the dream ended. It took about two years for me to understand fully what that all meant. Now I understand it well enough to make it workable. Through experience, testing, and a lot of reading, it finally all became quite clear.

The dream actually has two meanings. Here is the first.

Actions are the last component of the creation processes. It is a little like swimming competitively. You cannot win the Olympics if you only know how to thrash in the water vigorously and barely make it from one end of the pool to the other. You are acting, and very strongly. No one will fault you on your effort in the pool. You get full marks for effort, for sure. But the people who win gold medals are the ones who prepare their spirits. Their being is prepared. They are confident, motivated, focused. Their minds are also prepared. Their technique is also prepared. They are rested and alert. And so on. Action in the pool is the most noticeable bit of their total winning package, but it is the final part of their creating that gold-medal-winning dash.

In your life, although you may not know it, you create your experiences first in your Self, spirit, being, then in your mind, then by your words, and finally by your actions. The process starts with being, then moves on to thinking, then to speaking, then to acting. In fact, acting only puts into place the system necessary to receive and experience what you create in being, thinking, and speaking.

Most people do not focus, nurture, and tend to the first three steps of being, thinking, and speaking; all they do is work like crazy all day and wonder why they are not "successful." They do not use the Word. The Word refers to the laws of the universe—the way the universe works, on all levels, not just the visible and physical. These laws are not some commandments from God. They are simply the laws that regulate and enable the universe. These are not just spiritual laws; they can be proven scientifically using quantum physics. The Word, these laws, has nothing to do with a particular religion or person or philosophy; the laws of the universe apply equally and unfailingly to everyone and everything at all times. They never err. These are laws like the law of cause and effect—called karma or reaping and sowing in spiritual teachings—or the laws of energy conservation in science.

Actions are part of the Word, the laws of the universe, but they are only a small component of it. It is important to know what role actions play and how to use them in creating wealth or anything else. Actions are important, for sure, but you must understand that they are the last step. Their role is to receive what you have already created on your other three levels. You create; then you receive your creations; then you experience them. Action is for receiving and experiencing. You create a business in your Self, your being, then in your thoughts and words, and then you act to set up a system to receive this business in a manifested physical way so that you can experience it. See? Action does not create. It only receives and experiences.

In fact, even when it comes to experiencing, your actions don't create the experience—your mind does. Action just helps your mind to "do" the thing, then your mind decides: Will I experience this positively? Negatively? Joyfully? Fearfully? Fast? Slow?

Now let us look at the second meaning of my dream. This part actually goes beyond even the creation of these laws of the universe. Even before the laws came, there was an origin. I will only summarize it here. Before anything was created—anything at all—there was an infinite void (called the darkness in the Bible), a field of infinite potential, a field of No Thing. Out of No Thing, nothing and something arose. Even nothing needed a container, an originator, and that originator was No Thing, the Infinite Eternal Void. Now, the very first thing to arise out of that Infinite Void, that Infinite Undisturbed Peace, was a vibration. An instance of a vibration. For a reason we do not know, something awoke in that void, first by a small vibration. And then it happened again. And again, growing, exciting the next, and so on.

In the beginning, there was the Word, the vibration, a tiny infinitely small particle. An awareness, consciousness, creation. And as it grew, it shone even brighter, clearer, and started to create more like itself by exciting the void with intent, extending itself. Forever. Although they are all equal, the ones that came after are forever linked to and nourished by the First One. And the First One is forever the Universal God. In the beginning, there was the Word, the vibration. And the Word was with God, and the Word was God. That is how creation works, and it cannot work any other way. Therefore, it applies to you, because you are an extension of the original—your Self, your spirit, your soul is made in the image and likeness of the original.

So how does all this work? Look at it again. Then remember all we have learned about quantum physics. The first step in the creation of anything is your vibration. Remember that everything vibrates, and it is by that vibration that we harmonize and attract experiences to our selves. Consciousness, in a sense, is a vibration. Happy conditions arise because you are happy, and not the other way around. Wealth comes to you because of your wealth consciousness. So before you act or do anything at all, first ask yourself: "How am I vibrating?" And how do you tell how you are vibrating? You tell by how you feel. Your feelings show you your vibration. So how do you feel in relation to money? How you feel determines what you attract to you. You are like one huge radio with a tuning knob, and you can tune into any experience simply by matching your feeling to it. Action is a necessary step, but the last step nevertheless. It cannot be used effectively to initiate, as initiation is the function of being, followed by thought.

Know all this, and you will stop thrashing about in the pool.

Always do an excellent job. Always focus on the task and produce excellent value from it. Do this no matter how small the action seems. Even the smallest action has the potential to be the cause of the greatest next opportunity for you. In this universe, absolutely everything is a cause for another thing and is caused by something else. Even your smallest action may cause a previously unrevealed big thing that you need. Even an action as small as a smile or good service can cause the establishment of a relationship and the opening of doors that you never thought possible.

—I am wealth. I am abundance. I am joy.—

Ideas are worthless without action.

—I am wealth. I am abundance. I am joy.—

Action makes it possible to receive what is coming your way from your intentions. Intention initiates the creation of wealth; action enables the reception of it. Take action.

—I am wealth. I am abundance. I am joy.—

Even the smallest action may be what is needed to move you on to great wealth. Everything counts; every act counts and every act defines your next world. The universe is one huge chain reaction.

—I am wealth. I am abundance. I am joy.—

Do not try to do anything. Just do it. Or do not. But do not ever just try. Either you set out to do something, or you do not do it; but never set out to try to do it. If you try to do something, the universe will try to give you a result. But if you just do something with a resolve that it will be done (not "it may work out," but "it will work out"), the universe will honor that resolve and give you back its own resolve.

—I am wealth. I am abundance. I am joy.—

You already know how to do the things that you are not doing. If you are making $100,000 a year, you know how to take that to $1 million. If you sit and think it through, you will realize that you have some plans, some clues, that can get you there, or at least get you started on a path that will get you to that higher income level. In other words, you cannot possibly say truthfully: "I do not know what the first thing is that I should do to increase my income." It is not possible. At the very least, you have a clue about the first step, however small it may be; and that is all you need to start. The rest will reveal itself to you as you move on. But if you are not acting on that first clue or step, you'll never get to the next step. Bridge the gap now, by doing what you know, now. Start now. Just do it. The next step will become clear and available after you take the first.

—I am wealth. I am abundance. I am joy.—

If you are not in a perfect business, do not wait until you are. Start now in the one you are in and move gradually to the one you wish to have. This is the same with location, knowledge, and everything else. Start now; do not wait until things are "perfect" before you act.

—I am wealth. I am abundance. I am joy.—

Stop reacting and start creating.

—I am wealth. I am abundance. I am joy.—

As if. Act as if you are already the person you want to be. Act as if it is impossible not to get where you wish to go.

—I am wealth. I am abundance. I am joy.—

Opportunities increase as they are taken.

—*Sun Tzu*

—I am wealth. I am abundance. I am joy.—

Take advantage of the opportunity most available to you now, and it will open up previously hidden paths to more opportunities. By the law of cause and effect, your taking advantage of the opportunity closest to you will cause the unfolding of many more opportunities previously unavailable to you.

—I am wealth. I am abundance. I am joy.—

All other things held constant, to the extent that an individual or society has positive and grand actions in the right way, so will it have wealth and happiness.

As you can see, acting is not difficult. In fact, it is the easiest part of creation. In the past, it has been overemphasized, but as you can see, it is the last step in a very big system. This alone—ignoring the previous steps to acting—can explain a lot about why many people are not as wealthy and happy as they wish to be. Now you know.

But always remember that acting is very important in the chain of events, even if it is not the start of the chain. Do not now ignore it. The way to wealth and happiness is the way of perfect balance. Balance your body, mind, and soul. Balance the time and emphasis you give to being, thinking, speaking, and acting—don't just act all day long and do little structured thinking and visualization, for example. Nor should you spend all your time on spiritual nutrition and ignore acting and everything else. That would not only be selfish; it would also fail to complete the cycle of creation.

Now that you have the full set of creation tools with you, let us look at the fuel that makes them work. The tools of creation are just that—tools. They need one last ingredient to work—an ingredient so powerful that no other force can equal it.

CHAPTER 9

Certainty: The Most Powerful Force and the Antidote to Failure

CERTAINTY, FAITH, BELIEF, is a necessary part of creating wealth—or anything else for that matter. It is that which gives the universe a go-ahead to do as you wish it to do. You see, you cannot become a state without certainty, for such becoming is unbecoming. You cannot be happy if you are unsure that you are happy. You also cannot create goals without being certain, not only of their accuracy, but also of their coming to reality for you. Even speaking and acting without certainty is powerless.

Many teachers in many religions in many ages have taught us to have faith, to be certain. This isn't new. But now you will see why they have always taught this, and see how to create and expand your faith—something that has, so far, been elusive to many people.

But remember, as you read on, that faith is a lot like a state, or being. You cannot really *speak* faith; you can't *do* faith. You can only *be* faithful, *be* certain. And the way to do that is simply to decide to be certain—just like that—and let no other contradictory thought come to you. As we proceed, this will get easier and clearer.

The last part of getting faith is to understand how the universe works. In other chapters (on quantum physics, time, and cause and effect), you will see how the universe works, and this will give you faith because you will know exactly what happens behind the scenes. Once you understand how it all works, you will believe.

Everything is possible to the extent that you are certain.

To the extent that you have faith and clarity of thought, things are possible or impossible. But in reality, nothing is impossible.

—I am wealth. I am abundance. I am joy.—

Believe. Actually, be certain.

—I am wealth. I am abundance. I am joy.—

Persistence breeds faith. You can use persistence to increase your faith. And through faith, you have persistence. By persisting, even when it looks as if you should give up, you can increase your faith in an outcome and bring it about. This is a conscious decision you make, because faith enables persistence. It is a tight circle. You cannot achieve much if you are persistent but keep telling yourself that things are not going to work out. Persistence is a slight step ahead of faith, in that you can use it to build faith. But every step that persistence takes has to be followed by a step in faith. Persistence, literally, pays. Nothing is truly impossible.

—I am wealth. I am abundance. I am joy.—

Remove all thoughts of doubt and fear. Never entertain them, even for a moment. Be mindful, watchful, and aware of your thoughts by simply deciding to be so. Whenever you catch yourself doubting or fearing, stop those thoughts in their tracks; do not let them progress. Do not encourage them, but do not resist them. Instead, watch them mindfully and in a detached way, like an uninvolved watcher.

See what they are, where they come from, why they come to you, and how long they last. By observing them in this way, you will be able to get behind them, get to their cause, their dark origins. You will bring light to them, and eventually eliminate them.

—I am wealth. I am abundance. I am joy.—

Doubt and fear are the only enemies of your dreams and visions.

—I am wealth. I am abundance. I am joy.—

Certainty. Even in the face of contrary evidence, be certain, believe, have faith.

—I am wealth. I am abundance. I am joy.—

If you can? Everything is possible for him who believes.
—Jesus Christ, Mark 9:23

—I am wealth. I am abundance. I am joy.—

Confidence. Certainty. Believe it all the way, unquestioningly. In God's world, certainty is the only thing that will do. This is the stuff of miracles. This force moves mountains.

—I am wealth. I am abundance. I am joy.—

Doubt, confusion, fear, and worry have their roots partially in a person not knowing exactly what he or she wishes to be and have.

—I am wealth. I am abundance. I am joy.—

The opportunities and abilities that you have right now, right here, are enormous and incalculable. In other words, you cannot run out. Your belief is your only real limit.

—I am wealth. I am abundance. I am joy.—

As you believe, so shall it be done unto you. In the real sense, it is not that God rewards those with faith. What happens is that the universe moves its own building blocks—quantum particles—around depending on the information it receives and the certainty of that information. It is as scientific as it is spiritual.

—I am wealth. I am abundance. I am joy.—

Fear is false evidence appearing real. In reality, there is absolutely nothing to be afraid of, for your Self has it all and is indestructible. Your Self is designed never to lack anything, for it has it all already. It is also indestructible. But its manifestation here on earth comes with many illusions, and one of your purposes here is to overcome these illusions. One of those illusions is the illusion that abundance does not exist. Yet we know scientifically (thanks to quantum physics) and spiritually (as we have been advised by teachers throughout the ages) that abundance is All There Is. If you ever catch yourself fearing something, know that it is an illusion, and seek to find out what that illusion is. For in reality, there is nothing to fear at all.

—I am wealth. I am abundance. I am joy.—

Being broke is temporary. And it carries with it some immense lessons and opportunities for positive change. Do not fear going broke. It is not necessary to go broke, but if you find yourself broke, do not worry about it. Look for the lessons and opportunities in it. Fear of going broke is a terrible disease. It takes away opportunities for growth; it prevents people from trying new things; and it keeps them worried. Fear also attracts that which is feared, and the fear of poverty creates poverty. Yet, there is nothing to be afraid of except the fear itself.

—I am wealth. I am abundance. I am joy.—

When you most feel like holding on to something, it is usually the best time to let go.

—I am wealth. I am abundance. I am joy.—

Have faith. Believe. Know with certainty. When you pick up a glass of water to drink from it, you know without a shred of doubt that you will pick it up and drink it. The thought does not even occur to you that you may not be able to drink the water. You do it with certainty. That is the level of faith, belief, and certainty you should have in yourself, in the laws of the universe, and in the capabilities of the Source to work perfectly all the time. It is the certainty you should have about your having received even before you asked, and in the guarantee that you have it All. If you think you do not have something, decide, Now, that you have it, and you will. Do not say: "But I don't have it." Do not negate. Over time, it will become second nature. Until then, do your best and never think you cannot have it. Mind your mind. You can acquire faith with practice. But it is faster just to decide once and for all that you have it. How? Just decide.

—I am wealth. I am abundance. I am joy.—

How much faith, belief, and certainty should you have? You should have that which is at the level of knowing. You just know it to be true, just as you know that you woke up today or that you drank that glass of water earlier. At that level, you are so clear that something is true and will happen that you continue to be certain of it even if something contrary appears to you in the physical world.

—I am wealth. I am abundance. I am joy.—

This is the triad of knowing how to have whatever you like:

- Ask and it shall always be given to you;

- Seek and you shall always find it;

- Knock and it shall be opened unto you.

But there is one catalyst that must be there for this triad to work—belief, for belief makes all things possible. These are not empty promises. They are not rewards given to nice people only. It is the way the entire universe works without fail or exception. This triad and its catalyst can also be written this way: Desire and intend, and you shall always have it. Quest for the truth and knowledge, and you shall always know what you seek to know. There are no real boundaries to your growth, for you are more than welcome to experience any choices you make. But you must be certain that these statements are true, for if you believe they are not true or they are only partially or selectively true, that is exactly what you will get.

—I am wealth. I am abundance. I am joy.—

When in doubt, act your way into belief. If you are not confident, act as if you were, and that will make you confident eventually. Do this with everything about which you are not confident and your circle of confidence will begin to grow and encompass more and more aspects of life.

—I am wealth. I am abundance. I am joy.—

Persistence pays, literally. It also strengthens you and reinforces your belief. Persist. Persist. But in your persistence, let things happen. Let life work out. Do not worry. Be detached.

—I am wealth. I am abundance. I am joy.—

Not clearly knowing what you wish to have is a major cause of doubt and disbelief.

—I am wealth. I am abundance. I am joy.—

Faith is the external elixir which gives life, power and action to the impulse thought! Faith is the starting point of all accumulation of riches! Faith is the basis of all miracles and all mysteries which cannot be analyzed by the rules of science! Faith is the only known antidote for failure!

—Napoleon Hill

—I am wealth. I am abundance. I am joy.—

You can think and talk yourself into faith. Right now, people who continuously worry about things are thinking and talking themselves into doubt. To create faith, repeat, repeat, and repeat positive affirmations to yourself—every day, all day—and your subconscious will eventually believe.

—I am wealth. I am abundance. I am joy.—

Fear is false evidence appearing real. It always is. It is not your natural state. The state of the Source and of your Self is fearlessness, for there is nothing that can threaten the Self and nothing that the Self lacks. Whenever you fear, look it in the eye and find the false evidence—there is always some.

—I am wealth. I am abundance. I am joy.—

Never worry. Worry is fear, false evidence appearing real, putting images in your mind. Life is images in your mind expressed. Worry and fear put negative images in your mind and create that which you worry about and fear—an illusion that becomes real to you and becomes physical eventually if perpetuated.

—I am wealth. I am abundance. I am joy.—

Worry is a lack of all the facts needed in a particular situation. It is also the absence or suspension of certainty. It is misdirected and wasted energy.

—I am wealth. I am abundance. I am joy.—

The best way to heal fear and worry is to face it and analyze it fully; break it down into its components and see where the false evidence lies. Become aware and keep raising your awareness in finer detail. This raises your confidence as you uncover truth and that wipes out fear.

—I am wealth. I am abundance. I am joy.—

Observe truly what works and what does not, and live the truth by doing what observably works. Observe the truth; know the truth; think the truth; speak the truth; live the truth. This speeds up results and keeps fear away.

—I am wealth. I am abundance. I am joy.—

You now know about the laws of the universe that never err, and you will know more about them in later chapters. You know that these laws guarantee exact results when given a detailed, clear, consistent image and intention backed by certainty and action. You know that these laws work with infinite intelligence that you cannot possibly predetermine. And you know that you should never look at the physical and allow that to determine your thoughts, because it is thoughts that create the physical. Given all this, why in the world would you ever worry? Look at these statements again, slowly, in their parts. You will see that there is absolutely no reason to worry.

- Before any problem even occurs, it is solved.

- Before you ask, it is given.

- Everything that can possibly exist already exists, right Now, including all your potential "problems" and their solutions. All you do is shift your consciousness to experience portions of it as you make choices.

- The biggest lessons and opportunities for your self-evolution come through your worst times (because suffering is an indication of wrong thought). At such times, all you need to do is learn, see where the wrong thought is. Once you make the corrections, the fruits are fantastic.

Why then would you worry? There is no reason at all! The universe never makes mistakes. Chaos is in our minds only; it is not a property of the universe. Again, if the universe runs on certain laws, and these laws never fail, and you learn these laws and apply them, why would you ever worry? After all, you can predict an outcome based on your application of these laws. Worry only attracts to you what you worry about. Worry is a self-fulfilling prophecy.

—I am wealth. I am abundance. I am joy.—

I tell you the truth, if anyone says to this mountain, "Go, throw yourself into the sea," and does not doubt in his heart but believes that what he says will happen, it will be done for him.

—*Jesus Christ, Mark 11:23*

—I am wealth. I am abundance. I am joy.—

Whatever you believe, you can do. Whatever you wish for believing you have it, you shall have it. In other words, you are always having what you believe in truly. Think about that. You are always having what you believe in truly, to the extent that you believe. The rule never breaks.

—I am wealth. I am abundance. I am joy.—

All other things held constant, to the extent that an individual or society has positive and grand certainty in the right way, so will it have wealth and happiness.

Now you have the tools of creation and the energizing force that gives them life. Always be in a state of certainty and refuse to be in any other state contrary to certainty or think any thoughts that are contrary to faith. It is now time to move on to larger workings of the universe—the "fields" and laws within which you will use your tools and certainty. The first of these is the law of cause and effect—a beautiful promise that allows you to be guaranteed of effects and to figure out the causes of everything in your world. You always wished to know why things happen, and how you can make things happen. The first step to knowing is to study the law of cause and effect in order to see the truth about conditions and conditionality. Let's begin to look under the hood of what you see around you, what you experience.

CHAPTER 10

Cause and Effect: The Prime
Law of the Universe

THE LAW OF CAUSE AND EFFECT is the most important law of the universe. It is a prime key to wealth consciousness. If you live by this law, you cannot fail to get wealth. Understanding and living by the law of cause and effect guarantees that you shall not fail to cause the events you wish to experience—that you shall predict outcomes and figure out the causes of your situations. Simply learn this law well and read the chapters on conditions and success, and you will be well on your way to wealth and happiness. Wealth is created when you correctly plug your tools of creation, powered by faith, into the law of cause and effect.

The law of cause and effect is the prime law that runs the universe. It is the #1 law. Every spiritual and scientific teacher has sought to teach it, although they may have said it in a number of different ways: you reap what you sow, or you get what you give, or what goes around comes around, or karma, or consequences, or every action has an equal and opposite reaction, or many other similar statements. Quantum physics is now teaching us how this works, exactly, on a subatomic level.

Here is what we are now discovering: it is multiplicative! In other words, you will not only one day experience what you cause others to experience or its equivalent; you will do so multiplicatively! If you cause others to experience wealth and happiness, it will come back to you and you will experience it as well. But as a bonus, you will experience much more than you caused others to experience. Life is about growth. This is so for every experience imaginable. At some point in the complex of the space-time continuum, at some point in your life, by law, you experience a multiple of what you cause others to experience. Nothing escapes this law. Even if you cannot see where this is happening with your limited five physical senses right now, know that it happens and use it to create massive wealth.

Scientists now agree that nothing can be observed without being affected by the observer. In fact, they have concluded that even their experiments must be done in a double-blind fashion to get anywhere close to accuracy, because their own expectations affect the outcome of the experiments. And even double-blind rigor cannot create a completely independent experiment, because the thing being observed is created and recreated by the observer. Scientific evidence, especially in quantum physics, shows that you are the cause for all that you see in your world.

—I am wealth. I am abundance. I am joy.—

Cause others to experience wealth massively, increase their wealth consciousness massively, and you will experience wealth massively. Look at life today. Any business that deals with increasing people's productivity and connectivity always becomes a very big self-sustaining business. It may not be a perfect business, but it will be big and self-sustaining. Software, networks, transport, electronics, and similar businesses improve people's productivity and standard of living, and in return, they grow. But that is only a scratch on the surface. Even more magnificence will come our way when we start building businesses that are deliberately designed to give rather than receive—businesses designed to make other people wealthy. Future businesses will be designed to cause growth that is true growth and not growth with serious side effects somewhere else. These businesses will elevate populations from a lower standard of living to a higher one, and will elevate their consciousness and well-being as well. The more you cause others to have wealth, the more you will have wealth, effortlessly.

—I am wealth. I am abundance. I am joy.—

Whatever you wish to get, give it away first. This is the fastest path. Whatever you wish to have, cause another to have it first.

—I am wealth. I am abundance. I am joy.—

What you reap, you will sow. Karma. The law of cause and effect. This law never fails, and since, eventually, you always harvest what you sow, it is always in your best interests to sow good seeds. Do not be unjust to anyone unless you wish to have injustice turned back to you one day. Hate, covetousness, greed, anger are all negative thoughts and actions that cause the negative conditions and suffering needed to bring about a correction in that negative thought. Remember always that the entire universal system is one, One, even though it appears separate. You will see this to be true as you read this book. What you do unto others is what you literally end up doing to yourself.

—I am wealth. I am abundance. I am joy.—

By knowing the cause-and-effect power of thought, you can accurately predict the future by looking at the thought of now. Fortunately, we have the power to change thoughts and alter the future.

—I am wealth. I am abundance. I am joy.—

Cause and effect. Karma. You reap what you sow. We have been given this message from various sources over the years, and it is true. It works without fail, and ignoring this law is the cause of much of our suffering and poverty. It is so simple. Simply be deliberate and thoughtful about what you are being, doing, thinking, or saying. Know that everything is a cause that has an effect. Then ask yourself: "This thing that I am being, thinking, saying, or doing, what is its probable effect?" The answer to that question is what you will reap later. So if you cause another to suffer, it will return to you at some point in life. Ignoring this law has caused much suffering for the human race. Following this law has caused much prosperity as well. There is no mysterious external force that causes you random and wanton suffering. There is no such thing as bad luck. It is all within you individually, and within the collective selves of your family, company, community, country, and world. Every single state of being, thought, word, and action was caused by something that came before it and will cause something that comes after it. When you wake up to this fact and ask yourself, "What caused that thought I just had?" or "What will be the effect of this thought I am having?" you can fine-tune your Self and align yourself with the universe. This is the path to experiencing wealth and abundance.

—I am wealth. I am abundance. I am joy.—

Things get better when you get better. They get worse when you get worse. The world is all within you. You are the cause of everything that happens in your life, whether you are conscious of it or not.

—I am wealth. I am abundance. I am joy.—

If you are the cause for everything in your world and so is everyone else for their world, it means that groups of people are collectively the cause of their collective world. Corporate success and "failure," neighborhood events, even wars and natural disasters all happen, not because of only one person in the group, but because of all the people collectively causing that by which they are collectively affected. This brings us to your business. You will get the fastest results if the people you work with and associate with are people of wealth conscious-ness. Which means that you should offer to help all those around you to improve their wealth consciousness. Remember also that one very powerful way of getting something is to cause another to get it. Couple these thoughts and you will see how widely beneficial it is for you to ensure that your employees, business partners, family, and even community and country and world—if they are interested— have ac-cess to educational material that allows them to build wealth con-sciousness in themselves.

—I am wealth. I am abundance. I am joy.—

Imagine you are on an island with just one other person, work-ing together for a whole year. Imagine that you are very friendly with each other, and that you talk and share the books and food your rela-tives send you. What would happen if you slapped that person? That person will either slap you back, find another way to harm you, stop sharing books and food with you, or just have a less friendly heart toward you even if he or she did not retaliate otherwise. Even if the other person does not seek revenge, some tension will build that will cut short the freedom and companionship you had. This simple ex-periment shows you that it is impossible for you to harm someone without getting it back in some form or another. You harm someone, and eventually you will hurt yourself. And if you can observe this to be so, why would you wish to harm someone? More appropriately, since when you harm someone else, you harm yourself, why would you wish to harm yourself?

Now, if you are working hard in your business, why would you wish to undo that work by harming others in and through your business, whether it is your customers, your employees, your suppliers, the society, or the environment? And following on what we shall soon see about collective consciousness and the results of it, why would you wish to be passive when people are harming others? You know you will be affected in a negative way eventually when you allow a large corporation and your government to do business oppressively and harmfully, so why would you let that happen while you sit on the sidelines, waiting for your negative share of the returns? To the extent that you allow other people's choices and consciousness to override your own, you will share in their consequences. To the extent that you determine and make your own choices about everything, you will enjoy your own consequences. Wealth follows these rules, as does everything else. Saying "I don't care" does not exempt you from the law of cause and effect.

Ask the people who were alive during World War II. If people had not said "I don't care, it's not my problem" from the very beginning, Hitler would never have gotten as far as he did, and those people would never had have to suffer the bombings and economic downturn caused by the war. To exist, Hitler needed the world's collective consciousness to say "I don't care, I am separate." If you really care about getting wealthy and staying wealthy, you had better start caring about the world, if only for your own sake.

—I am wealth. I am abundance. I am joy.—

Commerce that is not built on true mutual benefit leads to imbalance, lack of peace, and eventually war. Whether you are a person, a corporation, or a nation, if you are making super-profits at the expense of others, you will eventually, somehow, someday, end up harming yourself just as you harmed them. That is evident in the world and predictable by the law of cause and effect.

Peace is the biggest boost to prosperity, and it is in your own interest, for your own prosperity, to promote peace. One way to do that is to deal fairly in your own business and to seek to correct unfair trade practices around the world whenever you can. To the extent that you have peace, you will have prosperity. In other words, whatever level of prosperity you are in today, you would be more prosperous if you had more peace. This is true even for those in the arms business, as ridiculous as that may sound.

For example, the global military-industrial complex is one of the world's biggest consumers of national budgets. Every second and minute, millions of dollars are spent around the world on military expenditures. Yet this would be unnecessary if there were peace. Military expenditures do not circulate around an economy as most other expenditures do. They are largely dead funds. Look at all the expensive nuclear arms being destroyed now. Those millions of dollars spent every minute could instead have been spent on other activities that would actually be productive and circulate in the economy. Even if they were spent on guaranteeing the survival and equal opportunity of the poor and disadvantaged around the world, to give them a chance to build businesses instead of spending their whole day working just for a loaf of bread, the entire world would become more prosperous. It would be many times more prosperous. Imagine if the billions of people living in poverty became productive citizens with purchasing power. Wouldn't your business benefit? And this would be possible if military spending were directed instead to this cause. And those who benefit now from the arms trade would instead benefit from a different business in a world that is dozens of times more prosperous than this one.

Peace is prosperity; war is not. If you want living proof, look at the United States. Even the United States fought internal battles, until it united into one nation and stopped the disputes between its own states. Now it is prosperous largely because of its internal peace, cooperation, and free trade under almost-equal legal protection for all within its borders. The European Union is realizing this as well and seeking to do the same. So are many other initiatives around the world—in Asia, Latin America, the Middle East, Africa—all over, but to different extents and at different rates. So in your own dealings, promote peace through fair trade even when you have the opportunity to be unfair. And in the events of your community, country, and world see what you can do to promote fair trade and peace. It is for your own prosperity.

—I am wealth. I am abundance. I am joy.—

Nothing in your world is real. Nothing you see is real. It is an illusion created for your benefit so that you may experience your thoughts and state of being firsthand and purify them and make them better (that is why suffering is said to be an indicator of wrong thought). Being-ness, thoughts, words, and actions create your world. Change your mind and you change your world. Change your Self and you change your world.

—I am wealth. I am abundance. I am joy.—

Here is a shortcut to solving problems, including financial ones. Whenever you are faced with a confusing, unclear, or problematic situation, look at it and say, "I am that." And truly accept it, for you caused it and separation is an illusion. Then ask yourself, "Why am I that?" All confusion and fear will disappear, and solutions will automatically start to appear in the face of your "I am that" awareness. This applies to any situation, actually, not just to a problem.

—I am wealth. I am abundance. I am joy.—

Have you noticed how life works like a large complicated mirror? What you do to others, you do to yourself. If you wish to be happy, make others happy. If you wish to be free, make others free. Use this principle in your business, and you will be able to choose what you get back.

—I am wealth. I am abundance. I am joy.—

The linkages between all life and the system of cause and effect are extremely complex, efficient, effective, and transforming. An apparently extremely small cause can have a huge effect in the future (or in the past or present). Physicists have a beautiful way of explaining this simply. They call it the "butterfly effect." James Gleick, in his book *Chaos*, explains the butterfly effect as "the notion that a butterfly stirring the air today in Peking can transform storm systems next month in New York." And that is just a simple example. Everything is a cause that has an effect. And everything is an effect that had a cause. This is a huge chain reaction that is not bound by time, space, or form. In the case of wealth, the effect is either wealth or poverty. Be aware of your thoughts and their probable effects. Is a particular thought likely to lead to wealth or poverty? There are no such things as idle thoughts, words, actions, or states of being.

—I am wealth. I am abundance. I am joy.—

Do not feel guilty. Forgive yourself for past "failures" and choose to act correctly next time. But avoid guilt, as it is one of the biggest destroyers of focus and confidence. Do not dwell on the past. Forgive others also. You are not doing them a favor when you forgive them; you are doing yourself the favor. They will still have their own cause-and-effect (karmic) debt for all their actions whether you forgive them or not. But when you forgive them, you release yourself from a negative karmic cycle and release your energy for other positive things as well.

—I am wealth. I am abundance. I am joy.—

What is found in the effect is already in the cause. Try to understand this intimately. Then live deliberately.

—I am wealth. I am abundance. I am joy.—

Here is another interesting thing about cause and effect in regard to wealth. Why do you suppose people get inspiration to start a particular business or career or passion or hobby? Yes, they are the cause individually of their desires, but there is something else as well. The collective consciousness of this planet and universe also has a hand in causing this inspiration. Remember, life always manifests images of the mind and grants every sincere and certain desire without fail. And the mind field is One (your mind and all minds make up the unified mind field). So the reason you have an idea is partly that others have caused it. That is how supply and demand works behind the scenes. If a million more people suddenly desire and believe they can have a certain type of fashion accessory, for example, an appropriate person with the appropriate level of desire and belief to go into the fashion business will be inspired to create this fashion accessory and sell it to these people. Hence, all desires and beliefs will be fulfilled. The reason you have an idea is partly that others have caused it. When you visualize something you wish to have, someone is visualizing the same thing as something that they wish to give or sell.

So the next time you have inspiration, rejoice in knowing that a group of people, small or large, is actively asking you and waiting for you to fulfill their desires. In other words, somewhere around the world, people are praying very hard for just the thing you are inspired to do; you are the answer to their prayers. And they are the answer to yours. Everybody is an answer to a prayer—we are all gifts and miracles to each other, even though we may not immediately see how that is so. There is nothing to worry about except worry itself. You succeed—that is all you ever do.

An easy way to understand that everyone is a gift and that we all are responsible as one unified mind field is to think again of Hitler. How could Hitler have been a gift to us? First, realize that he would never have come to power without the acceptance of the world as a whole. The world created the conditions necessary for him to rise. And as he rose, the world said: "He is not our problem. We don't care what he is doing to those people over there as long as we are alright." This separatist ideology, coupled with the way our collective state of being had created a fertile state in which Hitler could grow and thrive, is what caused Hitler. He could not have done it alone, just one small person against the world. He needed the world's conscious and unconscious cooperation.

You cannot blame Hitler as a victimizer of the world without blaming the world as a creator of victimization conditions. Hitler allowed us to experience a negative aspect of ourselves. We are now a lot less likely to go into world wars. We know it is not a good idea. We are also less likely to ignore the plight of others, to act in unconcerned separatist ways. Hitler allowed us to correct, to a certain extent, the illusion of separation. All suffering comes from belief in an illusion. The truth sets you free. Everyone around you and everything that they do is a gift to you, allowing you to know and re-define yourself. You are the cause of your world.

Once you understand how a person as "bad" as Hitler can be a gift and how a person like him is caused by the world around him so that the world can experience its mind and beliefs, you will understand a big secret to wealth. Once you understand that Hitler acted as a mirror of the world, a focused collection of the little bits of indifference, small beliefs in superiority and separation in each person, you will understand how you can be the focused collection of wealth for the world. In other words, do not be afraid to dream big, to dream of grand wealth, and to believe you can have grand wealth. The world will make it happen, and it is in fact making you have those grand dreams to the extent that you are willing to have them. You are fully supported, whichever way you choose to go.

—I am wealth. I am abundance. I am joy.—

All other things held constant, to the extent that an individual or society understands and applies the law of cause and effect in the right way, so will it have wealth and happiness.

What you now have is a good introduction to the universe's prime law. As you read the remaining chapters, you will understand this law a whole lot more clearly, especially after reading the chapters on conditions, success, and quantum physics. Now that you are armed with knowledge of the law that runs the universe, let us have a look at what conditions and success truly are. You are about to enter into one of the most beautiful, forgiving, and encouraging journeys you have ever taken.

CHAPTER 11

Conditions: They Are Fantastic Illusions

ONCE HAD A RATHER COMPLEX DREAM in a language that was, well, symbolic—or maybe wordless would be the best way to describe it. It was one of those dreams you have when you are just almost waking up; when you are half awake/half asleep. I was well aware of what was happening. An orange wall appeared in front of my eyes, and I began to pay attention. Then, in a script that looked like symbols, yet which I could somehow read during the dream, "words" started to appear that said something like "Conditionality does not exist. It is created." This went on for quite some time. A knowing voice also read along, in a vibration-like language, as I watched and understood. The message was about five sentences long—very complete and sensible knowledge. It ended in seconds, and I quickly got up and pulled out my notebook to try to write down the exact words that were spoken. But the minute I started getting frantic and looking for a pen, I lost the exact words. In any case, their composition was not linear like the sentences in this book.

Nevertheless, I was able to keep the meaning even though I lost the exact wording. In this chapter, you'll read the essence of that message. It is a little easier to understand if you first understand the real nature of time and quantum physics. Once you fully understand time, you will also understand that it is a scientific illusion. Einstein and other brilliant scientists have shown us how the space-time continuum really works. We now see how everything—past, present, and future—all exists in an eternal moment of Now. But being little participants within this moment, we experience a sensation of time as we pass other participants in that continuum.

As we see in quantum physics, the quantum "soup" is quite literally all things and all options that can possibly exist existing all at once. In other words, everything you can possibly imagine and more exists already, and it exists at this moment of Now. Everything!

So a wealthy you and a non-wealthy you exist simultaneously, but you are experiencing only one of them—you are conscious, awake to, and aware of only one.

It is now time for you to put on your thinking cap.

Question: If everything exists all at once, right now, how can conditions exist as real properties of the universe?

Answer: They can't.

Question: If all possible outcomes exist, how can there be a condition against certain outcomes existing, when they already exist?

Answer: There can't.

Look, just a moment ago, you read the last sentence. You have already read it. How then can there be a condition that you have not read it when you have already read it? It is not possible. So because everything possible, everything conceivable, already exists, it is not possible for there to be a condition of its not existing.

Your being wealthy already exists—scientifically and spiritually. All you need to do is shift your awareness, your consciousness, to that part of your Self that is wealthy. There are no conditions to that part's existence—nothing can stop it from existing because it already exists. But you can create other outcomes that look like conditions. For example, another thing that exists, but that you may not be experiencing, is your not being wealthy, your procrastination or feeling out of time, your going to the casino and getting a gambling habit, your being in a poor country and having no education, and so on. All these are independent existences that are the opposite of wealthy existence. But just because they exist does not mean that the wealthy existence does not exist or exists depending on these other existences.

People make the mistake of saying: "Well, if I had been born into a wealthy family, or in a good country, or with this gift or that knowledge, or if I had gone to that college or had that thing happen to me, I would be wealthy." They assume that wealth has a condition. Yet what they call a condition is actually another independent existence. In other words, you can get to wealth with or without having to pass through the so-called condition. You do not need to fulfill these conditions to get wealthy. But when you believe in conditions, they will be there. There are countless paths to wealth, and conditions are just one of those paths; it is your choice whether or not you wish to go through conditions. Even time, which looks like a condition, is not. People think you need a lot of time and age to get wealthy, so it happens that way for them, but it does not have to be that way.

Everything that is conceivable exists; you can only understand this if you understand the nature of time, quanta, and spirit. Conditions are not if-then statements that separate having and not having. They are just another outcome out of an infinite number of outcomes. They do not exist as conditions; they exist as just another possible existence. You do not have to pass through them; but if you believe in conditions and you create them, then of course you will experience them.

The important thing to know is that, even scientifically, conditions do not exist as if-then statements, as requirements that you have to go through, or as traps that you are born in and must stay in, or as things you can only get out of by performing certain actions or getting external help. Conditionality does not exist. We have designed conditionality on our own. What you call a condition is not a condition; it is just another one of infinite possible existences, and it does not exclude you from having another existence.

Read on, and you will understand conditions, and then overcome them. Conditionality does not exist.

Outside circumstances can only affect you as far as you allow them to do so.

—I am wealth. I am abundance. I am joy.—

The outer environment and conditions of a person are always related to the person's inner states and thought. It is through the environment and conditions that we experience and discover our thoughts and states. This is made possible by the fact that the universe, without error, fashions the environment and conditions we experience from our thoughts and states of being. We are always in the perfect setting to see and experience ourselves, to change and grow. It is in recognizing and using this perfect system that we can direct and quicken our growth in wealth and all other areas.

—I am wealth. I am abundance. I am joy.—

Think outside the box—the box that has been created by your past conditioning, experiences, teachers, news, environment, and so on. It is not a real box; it only exists in your mind and the minds of

A Happy Pocket Full of Money

those around you. This is all that keeps the box there. It is not real on its own; it needs you and everyone else to survive.

You can break out of the box by thinking outside it. You have heard this many times, but now you can finally do it all the time. You do it by dropping all constructions you have in your mind as to how to do things. For example, some people who have never had a university education believe that, to be wealthy, you have to have a university degree. They were told that, and they think they may have observed that, so they hold it to be true. But this limitation can be removed simply by dropping that construction and belief in it from all thought. Many have dropped it and succeeded wildly. In fact, Bill Gates of Microsoft voluntarily dropped out of college; he just never did finish that undergraduate degree. And millions around the world have succeeded wildly without a college degree. This is not to say that you should not go to university. Universities have a very important role to play. But if you find that your "box" is that you have not been to university and you are unable to go there, simply drop the construction and your belief in it, and your box will disappear. That is thinking outside the box.

You can do this in anything, from product development, to finance, to new business ideas, or anything else. You do it merely by being aware, intending to do it, and consciously dropping your constructions.

> **Question**: How do you build a totally new and radical house or car?

> **Answer**: By dropping all previous constructions of how you have been told a house or a car needs to be built.

Drop it all and have a clean slate without any "shoulds" and "should nots." Then drop the slate! Let it all come to you. Inspiration unrestricted by "should" or "should not" is key. It is a very deliberate, yet unbound, thing to do. And very fruitful. Ask Einstein.

—I am wealth. I am abundance. I am joy.—

Make all conditions serve you, for that is what they are here to do. They are an experiential field created wholly for your enjoyment, self-discovery, and learning. This is because they are fashioned out of your previous thoughts, words, actions, and states of being.

—I am wealth. I am abundance. I am joy.—

Face all financial and other difficulties calmly and without worry. Even before they occurred, they had been solved. Even before you ask, it has been given to you. Simply receive.

—I am wealth. I am abundance. I am joy.—

There are no coincidences or accidents, no chance or luck in this universe. The universe works under perfect laws that never make an error even once. The Source, God, does work perfectly. Everything works out perfectly by law. Things only look like coincidences and accidents to those who do not see the truths behind them.

—I am wealth. I am abundance. I am joy.—

Nature works with effortless ease and precision, with infinite organizing power, in incalculable ways, without resistance. You do not have to understand how your wealth will be created. Simply hold your vision high—think, speak, and do by your vision—and automatically, "coincidentally," it will all work out. Do not resist whatever happens along the way, for it is only nature's incalculable way working to bring you what you envisioned. Just hold your end of the bargain by keeping your vision high and steadfast, and think, speak, and act according to your vision.

Be detached. This allows nature's creativity to work for you. Detachment means not preferring anything other than what is happening right now, but having the freedom to choose a different future. What is happening right now is the perfect manifestation of your previous intentions, thoughts, words, and actions. Preferring an alternative Now leads to delaying the achievement of your goals. Such preference is wanting, and wanting perpetuates a state of wanting.

For example, if it is your desire and intention to become a multimillionaire, and you have done your part in aligning your thoughts, words, and actions with your vision, you must admit that you do not know which is the best and optimal path for you to take to reach that goal. You cannot predict the exact day-to-day events that you need to lead you to your desired outcome. But the Source can do that easily. Your inner Self can do that as well. And it will take you there in the best way possible. Let it work its magical way by not resisting the moment of Now that it brings you. Just do your part, and let it do its part. It is the fastest, most effective, most enjoyable way. And you can be happy and restful always, for you know what is coming eventually.

—I am wealth. I am abundance. I am joy.—

Calmness is power. Calmness puts you in harmony with yourself and nature. It puts you in control of your thoughts and enables you to have right thought. It is a testament to the fact that you are not your circumstances and that you are not inferior to your circumstances. Calmness is confidence. Calmness is your true nature, perfect balance, perfect stillness, and perfect peace. Always say, "I am calm."

—I am wealth. I am abundance. I am joy.—

Calmness is not suppression. True calmness is clear and open; it does not hide or suppress anything internally in order to show calmness. It is pure and natural. Calmness represents, and can be developed by knowing, internalizing, practicing, and living the laws of the universe, the laws of life—laws like the ones in this book.

—I am wealth. I am abundance. I am joy.—

Suffering indicates an error in thinking. It is a cue for you to find and change that error. Often, in the deepest moments of suffering, you find the biggest opportunity to find new truth. But suffering is not necessary. In fact, the most enlightened of people have been able to eliminate suffering completely. Suffering is just a means for your Self to communicate with your personality and mind—and vice versa—and is only used when there are no other options. The people who are most resistant to more subtle clues from their Selves find themselves suffering the most. Those who are most aware and tuned to their Selves through things like active intuition are able to work out life deliberately instead of having life work them out.

—I am wealth. I am abundance. I am joy.—

Conditions do not exist. Conditionality is an illusion. Conditions are created to create an environment that matches your thoughts. In other words, conditionality is an illusion that follows thought to fulfill and manifest thought into experience of that thought. Conditions convert thought from symbols in the mind to actual experiences. The reality is that the universe contains all that there can possibly be, all held in the eternal moment of Now, Here. But if you believe and think that you are poor, conditions will form around you to fulfill that belief and those thoughts. On the other hand, if you believe and think that you are wealthy, conditions will form around you to fulfill that belief and those thoughts. Thus, the statement "I cannot afford that because I don't have the money" is false. What is actually happening is that you believe in insufficiency, and the world around you arranges itself over time to present you with "needs" of things that you "cannot" afford. By the way, for the same reason, need is also an illusion. How can you need what you already have? And you have it all, for it is all created. Even before you ask it has been given unto you, as Jesus and many other teachers have told us before and quantum physics is showing us now.

—I am wealth. I am abundance. I am joy.—

Conditions do not exist. Conditionality is an illusion. You cause conditions, yet it seems as if they are placed upon you by external forces. This is one of the most liberating insights. Understand it deeply. Live by it, make all your decisions by it, and life will become magic. Just try it.

—I am wealth. I am abundance. I am joy.—

When you fight against circumstances, you are fighting fruitlessly against effects, and strengthening and preserving the cause. Let us say, for example, that your circumstances are such that you see yourself as broke. If you act from a "broke" perspective (cutting costs, being mean and stingy, being bitter, scared, and jealous) in an attempt to prevent yourself from becoming even more broke, what are you really doing? Can you start to see how you are perpetuating and energizing the "broke" conditions? By consistently believing and thinking about being broke, you are creating the conditions of being broke, through the power of belief and thought. Remember, the universe always gives you what you think about most often, earnestly and with conviction. It is at your command. The way to fix being broke is to take on a state of wealth internally and think, speak, and act from that perspective.

—I am wealth. I am abundance. I am joy.—

Wealth is first a state of being, which is then experienced. It is not the other way around. Wealth is not created because of certain conditions. Certain conditions are created because of wealth.

Abundance is not created because of certain conditions. Certain conditions are created because of abundance. Conditionality does not exist. The following statement is wrong: A person is poor because of certain conditions around him or her. The following statement is right: Conditions of poverty are around a person because that person's Self and thoughts are of poverty consciousness. The state, being-ness, creates the conditions. Most people think it is the other way around. Those who see it clearly find their conditions magically transforming themselves to give them "lucky breaks" and "coincidences."

—I am wealth. I am abundance. I am joy.—

Get out of the thinking that you are your conditions. Say: "I am not my seeming lack of the wealth I wish to have. I am not my job. I am not my condition."

—I am wealth. I am abundance. I am joy.—

Why do things repeat themselves? Some people keep "failing" in whatever business they try, for example. Here is the reason: You keep bringing yourself the same circumstances and situations over and over again, until you decide to recreate yourself anew, change your thought pattern, and change yourself into a new, "improved" being.

—I am wealth. I am abundance. I am joy.—

Avoid judging things as right or wrong. Things are just things. Their classification lies in the choice of the observer of these things to classify them as good or bad, right or wrong, fun or not. The minute you judge things, you judge yourself. You also block the hidden gift that an event brings to you.

The Taoists have a wonderful way of explaining this using the story of the farmer whose horse ran away. A farmer's horse ran away, and his neighbor, feeling sorry for him, said to the farmer: "I am sorry that such a bad thing happened to you." The farmer replied: "Don't be, for who knows what is good or bad." Well, the next day, the horse that ran away came back to the farmer, this time bringing with it a herd of wild horses that it had befriended. The neighbor said to the farmer: "I congratulate you for your good fortune!" The farmer replied: "Don't, for who knows what is good or bad." Well, the next day the farmer's son tried to mount one of the wild horses and fell, breaking his leg. Again, the neighbor said to the farmer: "I am sorry that such a bad thing happened to you." The farmer replied: "Don't be, for who knows what is good or bad." The next day soldiers came by to forcefully recruit for the army, but the farmer's son was exempted because of his broken leg.

Now this is just a simple story, but it demonstrates the miracles that the Source works in the most unpredictable and seemingly unconnected ways so that all things work out to perfection. For those who know and work with the laws of the universe, those who apply the law of cause and effect, those who have certain goals and purpose and vision, this magic works beautifully, bringing with it synchronous events, "coincidences," and many other twists and turns that lead to the desired end.

So avoid judging things and people. It only slows you down and harms you. For you do not know the chain of events planned. Also, you become what you judge, and what you condemn returns to affect you. By the law of cause and effect, when you judge and condemn, you set yourself up to be judged and condemned. Your part is simply to have clear vision and certainty on all matters that relate to your life—the inner workings of how your visions and goals will come to be. The daily events, "good" or "bad," are taken care of for you, as long as you do not interfere with the process.

—I am wealth. I am abundance. I am joy.—

Your intention works like a magnet that draws to itself all that is needed to make it manifest into the physical world. Here is an example of how your intention works out. You think up a new idea; you have a new desire. You intend to have your desire come to life. This starts drawing to you all the things needed for you to attain your desire. It is a magical thing—you have certain dreams, you meet certain people, you go through certain conditions, you acquire certain skills— many seemingly coincidental events occur. As this process goes on, parts of your desire keep manifesting into reality until the whole of it completely manifests. Trust the system. Do not fight the things that are drawn to you by your intention, for they are the perfect drawings of your own co-creation.

—I am wealth. I am abundance. I am joy.—

See your predicaments with humor; this is the first step to getting unattached from them.

—I am wealth. I am abundance. I am joy.—

Why do people sometimes hit rock bottom? Why do people sometimes become devastated—financially, emotionally, or otherwise?

The answer lies in the way we use suffering. We are not designed for suffering. If we were to listen to our spirits a lot more, if we were to recapture that ability and be much more intuitive and listen to that intuition, our suffering would reduce dramatically. But when we refuse to listen to the higher wisdom of our souls, we suffer in the physical world so that we can correct errors in thinking. Haven't you ever wondered why is it that many of the people who become extremely wealthy had at some time been broke? The classic rags-to-riches story. Remember, it is not necessary for this to happen. But when it happens and the person it is happening to takes responsibility and learns from it, that person becomes very wealthy. At the bottom, at rock bottom, a person is stripped of everything. The false psychological defenses that keep that person from accepting his or her highest truth are taken away. When the person un-identifies with and disengages from these falsehoods and accepts the truth, he or she becomes wealthy.

One of the truths about wealth is that we are abundant by nature. There are many truths about wealth and happiness, and many are covered in this book. It is not necessary for you to go to rock bottom and suffer so that you may identify with the truth. Suffering only comes when people refuse to listen to more subtle signals. These signals can come from within or from sources like books, other people, TV, movies—the Source communicates in infinite ways. It is we who do not pay attention and listen. It is we who choose to ignore what we feel to be true.

Another reason for suffering is to teach us what not suffering is and how to get to a state of no suffering. For example, for you to know what red is, you have to know what red is not. You do not have to know this experientially and personally, but you definitely need to know it. Imagine a robot that has never experienced the state of happiness or sadness. This robot may be very smart, very well programmed in the knowledge of happiness and sadness. The programmer may "explain" as much as possible what happiness is. But that robot will only ever know conceptually what happiness is. And that is not true knowing; it is emptiness.

Only by experiencing happiness yourself can you know happiness. And to do that, you need to experience, even if only for a short while, the opposite of happiness, which is sadness. There are some things of which you need firsthand personal experience. And there are some things that you only need to know conceptually. Sometimes, the things you need to know firsthand include things you may call "suffering." But in essence, they are tools to enable you to enjoy their opposites, the very things that you seek.

—I am wealth. I am abundance. I am joy.—

Much of your pain is self-chosen. It is the bitter potion
by which the physician within you heals your sick self.
Therefore trust the physician, and drink his remedy in
silence and tranquility: For his hand, though heavy and
hard, is guided by the tender hand of the Unseen.

—*Kahlil Gibran*

—I am wealth. I am abundance. I am joy.—

The psychological rule says that when an inner situation
is not made conscious, it happens outside, as fate. That is
to say, when an individual remains undivided and does
not become conscious of his inner contradictions, the
world must perforce act out the conflict and be torn into
opposite halves.

—*Carl Jung*

—I am wealth. I am abundance. I am joy.—

**All other things held constant, to the extent that an individual
or society understands and uses the illusion of conditionality in the
right way, so will it have wealth and happiness.**

It feels refreshing to know that we are not at the mercy of some
random circumstances and conditions, to know that we create them and
they are beautiful gifts that come to serve our growth. It is liberating!

Now we shall look at an aspect of conditionality that has been
extremely misrepresented in society. They say that you can either succeed or fail. Here is the beautiful truth and secret: you always succeed.

CHAPTER 12

Success: You Can Never Fail

NO CONDITION CONCERNING WEALTH has been more misrepresented than success and failure. Many people think you can either succeed or fail. Well, failure is yet another illusion, and success is all that there is. This is such a profound truth that you should make every effort to understand it.

All of life is a success full of successive moments.

"Failure," when used without fear as a learning process, is what eliminates weakness and builds strength in thought and character. This new strength in thought and character is essential and critical to the future success that you seek. "Failure" is truly a successive moment, a moment of success in its own right. Through "failure," you learn how to succeed and what eventual triumph tastes like, for how would you know how to relish the sweet taste of triumph if you did not know how "failure" tasted? And how would you know how to arrive at your intended triumph without the tools designed to get you there?

—I am wealth. I am abundance. I am joy.—

The most common cause of "failure" is the lack of clear and focused goals and visualizations. The universe, life, literally lacks something to work with, so it does nothing. Life is images of the mind expressed. And without images, there is no expression.

—I am wealth. I am abundance. I am joy.—

Often, the greatest opportunity to be all that you can be lies in your darkest hour. Your worst moments are often your biggest liberators, your highest teachers. Do not fight and resist them when they come. Instead, look into them for the lessons they hold—the liberation they bring. Suffering is always an indication of an error in thinking. You are not designed to suffer. You were designed to enjoy life.

—I am wealth. I am abundance. I am joy.—

Gain and loss are two sides of the same thing. Through loss, you gain new things. Through loss, you know the sweetness of gain. Without loss, there would be no gain. It is the struggling against loss and the preference of gain over loss that causes suffering and retarded growth. It is the acceptance of both loss and gain as gifts and as fuel for your growth that will propel you to greater heights faster. In the end, you will see that loss was not really loss. At the point when you recognize the gains you got from the loss, you will see that the loss was really a blessing, and that loss does not exist. Every loss has a gain, if only you accept and look into it and have patience. Loss is usually the result of an error in your thinking, in which case you have the opportunity to correct your thoughts and make massive gains; or it is a new opportunity selected by your higher self designed to take you higher, a chance to discover a new, higher truth.

—I am wealth. I am abundance. I am joy.—

Use all conditions to enjoy and build yourself—that is what they are there for. Even the "negative" ones are useful. If, for example, you are faced with a situation in which you are under oppressive people, first make sure you choose to be in a liberated, self-loving, and loving state of being internally (the opposite of oppression). Think, speak, and act liberty, self-love, and love. Show your oppressors kindness and forgiveness, rather than being oppressive to them when you get the chance. That is how you get out of your negative circumstances, and by visualizing in detail, with belief, the way you wish to next create your world. When you become a non-oppressive person who loves yourself and others, truly, internally, you will find yourself leaving that oppressive situation. The negative situation will have done its work in "fixing" you, with your voluntary participation. Always remember that, at some level, whether you are conscious of it or not, you choose the circumstances you are in.

—I am wealth. I am abundance. I am joy.—

When you look within to find the error in thought causing your suffering, always look with humility so that your ego does not interfere. Look with sincerity to find truthfully. Look with no self-pity or mercy—call a spade a spade. Remember, it is a private exercise; no one else will know and ridicule you, so feel free to be precise and honest with yourself.

—I am wealth. I am abundance. I am joy.—

Most people have been programmed to fear failure. They give up to avoid failure, or they do not even attempt just so that they will not fail. Failure, however, is an illusion. Begin to see it as an illusion. Failure, suffering, is an essential component to success. It is what helps you correct wrong thought if you approach it with an attitude of learning. Through failure, you learn how to succeed. By trying and failing, you refine your thought and point it ever closer to success. But this is so only if you do not give up.

Through failure, you get to know success and how to get there. How else can you know what success tastes like if you do not know what it does not taste like? And how can you get there without knowing how? Think about that. Failure is an integral part of success. Failure is not the opposite of success, a separate entity from success. It is actually a successive moment that leads to ultimate success.

Failure is success. They are the same things, but on different ends of the spectrum of achievement—just like hot and cold are different ends of the spectrum of temperature on a thermometer. Failure and success are both different vibrations of the same thing.

Failure is not failure as such. It is only truly failure when you accept it as the end. But if you accept it as a blessed part of the process, a part that helps you succeed further and know what this further success tastes like, then you can never ever possibly fail, ever. Failure is an illusion. Stop fearing it; love it for the gifts it brings you.

—I am wealth. I am abundance. I am joy.—

Life is a collection of experiences. The challenges make up part of the experiences. Use the challenges to become better and enjoy the rewarding and triumphant experience that follows every challenge.

—I am wealth. I am abundance. I am joy.—

Every try is a success that leads to the eventual desired outcome, the big success. View it that way.

—I am wealth. I am abundance. I am joy.—

Your survival is guaranteed. You do not have to qualify for your dignity and life.

—I am wealth. I am abundance. I am joy.—

All other things held constant, to the extent that an individual or society encourages and applauds all moments, events, and attempts, seeing them as successive moments of successes, so will it have wealth and happiness.

Now that we have defined success and uncovered the illusion of failure, it is time to have a look at the object of the quest for success—in other words, what people want. Here is another secret: desire, but never want.

CHAPTER 13

Want Not: Desire—but Never, Ever Want

A S YOU HAVE SEEN, there is good reason to watch your words, thoughts, actions, and states. Every state and thought is acted upon precisely by the universe, by law. Each word carries with it thousands of years of meaning and instructions on how it will be carried out. For example, the word "jump" invokes specific images in everyone's mind, along with the appropriate instructions to execute it. And the universe, which has to assist in that jump, acts accordingly (laws of physics, spirit-mind-body coordination, etc). Even as you read this book, the words invoke in you certain things, some of which you can feel right now.

Some people by now will excitedly know that the words used here will enable them to make big differences in their lives. And that knowing is already starting to make changes unseen. And some people already know this as they read this.

In regard to wealth, the most important word to watch out for is *want* and all its equivalents. Wanting communicates to you and to the universe that you do not have something (first mistake) and that you are in a state of not having it but wishing you did (second mistake). The problem is compounded by the fact that wanting is a perpetual state. In itself, it has no finality. Think about it.

You can never get what you want. Never. It only looks as if people get what they want, but they never really do. What actually happens is that, very gradually, they shift from the state of wanting to other states and then they get what they wanted in the first place. But as long as they are in a state of wanting, they cannot get that which they want. Here is how the illusion of a person getting what they want works. Remember the last time you wanted to eat and you got what you wanted (you ate something). Okay, you wanted something to eat. This is a wanting state. But watch what happened next. You started to go get something to eat. You actually shifted from a wanting state to a getting state, which has finality. You then shifted to the present tense of having, finally, and you appear to have had what you wanted. See, you never did get what you wanted when you were in a wanting state. You had to shift states.

This unconscious shifting from a state of wanting to another state is easily done all the time—but only for small things. What if it were to happen for something really big, something you never had before? Would you still get it if you wanted it? Unlike food, it would be harder for you to shift unconsciously from the wanting state, because you have not gone through it before. If you found yourself wanting twenty dollars, it would be easy for you to shift unconsciously from the state of wanting it to the state of getting it, because you have done it before over and over. But what if you wanted a million dollars and you have never had more than $20,000 in your life? Would you be able to shift unconsciously from wanting to getting a million dollars? Most likely not. The solution is this: never want!

You can never get what you want. Wanting something very badly is worse. In your thoughts, words, states, and feelings, replace "want" with "desire" or "wish." Unlike wanting, desiring does not necessarily have to mean that you do not have something. It is a very subtle difference, and some people may say they are the same thing, but there is, in fact, a world of difference. Some thesauruses may even say "want" is interchangeable with "desire," but that is simply for linguistic purposes.

Remember, your thoughts are carried out with precision and perfection by the universe. It is the way the system is designed. Wanting is carried out with precision, and wanting represents a perpetual state of not having. Desire is not a perpetual state of not having; in fact, it does not necessarily have to mean you do not have what you desire. It is sad and funny to think that billions of people are kept away from what they want by such a simple little difference. It all lies in the precise execution of the universe.

More precisely, it is not just the word "want" that should be avoided. It is the state. It helps nothing to avoid the word "want" but be in a state of wanting—that is useless. Language is a symbol used to represent things like states. The word "want" is a symbol that represents the state of wanting. It is therefore the state that you should avoid first. The symbol, the word itself, is also to be avoided so as not to invoke the state. Please, desire, but never want.

Here is how the dictionary defines the word "want":

> to be without; lack. To be destitute or needy. A defect of
> character; a fault. To be absent; to be deficient or lacking;
> to fail; not to be sufficient; to fall or come short; to lack.

This is what you communicate to the universe when you want something. The universe brings you just that—absence and deficiency.

None of these negative definitions are included for the word "desire," however. Here's how the dictionary defines "desire":

> to express a wish for; request. The natural longing that is excited by the enjoyment or the thought of any good and impels to action or effort its continuance or possession; an eager wish to obtain or enjoy.

—I am wealth. I am abundance. I am joy.—

Not needing a particular result in the moment of Now frees your subconscious mind from all thoughts about why you cannot have a particular result. This, in turn, opens the path to the particular result that was consciously intended. This is one of the benefits of intending with detachment. You intend a future outcome. You are certain of it, but you are detached as to what is happening in the present moment. For example, assume that you intend to be a millionaire, but in the present moment, events are moving in a way that suggests you are not going toward your goal. You will make the best progress if you are detached about the present moment, meaning you accept it as it is instead of fighting it and getting frustrated by it and losing hope. But, regardless of your detachment, keep your certainty about your outcome (becoming a millionaire) in the future.

Learn to enable the co-existence of intention, certainty, and detachment in your life and life will quickly become happy and wealthy for you. Resistance and frustration will slowly fall away, and certainty and confidence will grow. You see, you cannot fail to get wealthy if your goals are clear and focused and you are certain and faithful, and you believe. It is impossible to fail. Failure would mean breaking the unbreakable laws of the universe. So certainty enables you to relax, knowing that wealth is on the way, regardless of whatever the present moment may look like. Lack of detachment equates to resistance, and what you resist persists.

—I am wealth. I am abundance. I am joy.—

Eliminate all forms of wanting. These include regretting the past, wishing things are or were different, looking forward to things, wishing, wanting, worrying, and throwing your awareness and consciousness out into the future or past. In other words, do not hold onto the past moment; do not wish you were in the next moment to come. Instead, take in the moment of Now in its fullness for all the gifts it brings to you. The fastest way to create a great future is simply to intend, release, and get back to enjoying Here, Now. Wanting tells the universe to create conditions that keep you in wanting, making it impossible to have what you desire unless you get out of the state of wanting and into another state. It is a very subtle, but important, way of seeing life.

—I am wealth. I am abundance. I am joy.—

Never want anything. Wanting makes the universe give you the conditions that create a perpetual state of wanting. Have passion, have desire, have intentions, but want not.

—I am wealth. I am abundance. I am joy.—

Eliminate the word "want" from your language and the state of wanting from your thinking and being. Replace it with "desire" and "desiring," "like" and "liking." Wanting creates conditions of perpetual wanting. You never get what you want.

—I am wealth. I am abundance. I am joy.—

If you ever find yourself thinking that you do not have something, or that you are not something, then you are wanting. Wanting is a state of being that professes not having, lacking. It is not just a word in the spoken language.

—I am wealth. I am abundance. I am joy.—

All other things held constant, to the extent that an individual or society eliminates wanting from its language and from its state of being, so will it have wealth and happiness.

If you find yourself fighting against want, reread the chapters on quantum physics, abundance, One, and self, and understand truly how, as it has been taught by many teachers for thousands of years, you have it all—even before you ask, it has been given to you. Logically, scientifically, and spiritually, there is absolutely no reason to want. Of course, there is reason to desire, but none to want. Wanting is a belief in not having. You have it all. Why then would you wish to believe that you do not have it?

Now that we have that all clear, let us look at some big and interesting things. We'll start with your purpose, that uniqueness of you that no one else can duplicate.

CHAPTER 14

Purpose: Why Are You Here?

WHAT IS YOUR PURPOSE? Your purpose is separate from your goals. What is your purpose; why are you here? Only by knowing and declaring your purpose and holding it high every day can you move forward quickly in the right direction for you, and have a great time doing so.

The right question is: Why did you choose to come here to earth?

Where did you get your purpose? Consider this suggestion. You have free will. When did this free will start? Some people think it starts when they are born. They believe that they did not have a choice whether or not to be born, but once they are here, they have free will to make choices in their lives.

Others believe that their free will is eternal, and that it starts even before they are born. That is not such a strange idea. Your soul is eternal. Your eyes tell you that life starts when you are born, but something deeper tells you that this may not be the real beginning. Purpose or destiny is what you, your Self or soul, choose to come do here on earth—a choice based on your soul's attributes and wishes. And the circumstances and location you are born in are perfect for you to collect the necessary "tools" to fulfill your chosen purpose were you to go through life with such an awareness. That is why your unique purpose feels so good once you find it. That is why it gives you so much joy doing it—because you chose it a long time ago. It is what you came here to do.

Unfortunately, many people do not fulfill their purpose, largely because of the way our society and educational system is structured. Yet you can easily fulfill yours if you choose to. First find your purpose by spending some quiet time thinking what makes you feel good, what you have passion for. Do not think of job descriptions or careers. Drop all those labels society has taught you to believe in. They are the #1 reason why people do *not* find their purpose. Just ask yourself: "What am I happy doing?" It may be spending time with butterflies or flying around the world making deals or cooking or speaking to people or anything else. Once you find your purpose, envision it, intend it, and make goals that move you toward it—to a point where you will be working, as a career, in your discovered purpose.

For example, imagine that your purpose is studying butterflies, and you are now working unhappily in a non-butterfly-related job. Do not despair. Start by getting books and finding people in the butterfly field. Find out all you can. Then start making goals and choices that will eventually take you out into a position that is butterfly-related. Do not worry about money and forget about all the other little worries you may start having; they will sort themselves out as long as you do not worry. And you will be very happy and successful once you work in your destiny or purpose, a destiny that you yourself chose before you were born here on earth. Your self-satisfaction will also rise, and you will be making an optimal contribution to the world at large.

—I am wealth. I am abundance. I am joy.—

Sit down quietly and find out why you are here. You have a purpose. You may or may not know it yet. You can discover what it is by asking yourself and by being true to yourself. Your special talent is usually your purpose. Or it may be something you always felt, especially as a child, that you could do very well. Children often know their purpose, but as they grow up, society and the educational system confuse them. Or your purpose may be what gives you most joy. In fact, your purpose cannot be something that does not give you joy and satisfaction. When you find it, live your life by it, and wealth will come to you a lot more easily and joyfully. And you will love your work.

—I am wealth. I am abundance. I am joy.—

Work is love made visible. And if you cannot work with
love but only with distaste, it is better that you should
leave your work and sit at the gate of the temple and
take alms of those who work with joy.
                                                    —*Kahlil Gibran*

—I am wealth. I am abundance. I am joy.—

Define your purpose in life clearly. Keep it high in your thoughts at all times. Declare your goals by it. Align your thoughts, words, and actions with it at all times, and your life will be fulfilled and satisfying.

—I am wealth. I am abundance. I am joy.—

The surest way to enjoy your work is to work within your purpose in life. Work within whatever you determine is your purpose in life, not your job or obligation, but that which you feel called from within to do, that which you dream of doing—and joy at work will be easy to experience. What does that tell you? That everyone can work at a job or business that they enjoy as long as they know what their purpose is and they work within it.

—I am wealth. I am abundance. I am joy.—

When you align your thoughts fearlessly to your life's purpose, you become a powerful creative force.

—I am wealth. I am abundance. I am joy.—

When you are working within your purpose, work is no longer a job; it becomes a pleasure, and it becomes life. The boundary between work and fun vanish.

—I am wealth. I am abundance. I am joy.—

How many purposes do you have? You have as many as you feel that you have. You are not restricted to just one. You are a multi-dimensional being.

—I am wealth. I am abundance. I am joy.—

All other things held constant, to the extent that an individual or society finds and works in their purpose, so will it have wealth and happiness.

Life is a celebration, and joy makes for celebration. Joy is spirit being expressed in the ways it likes and desires. Purpose gives spirit that opportunity. Find the purpose that you chose for yourself, and you will find love, joy, and wealth in your work and contribute optimally to society.

Speaking of contributions, did you know that one of the most powerful ways to get wealth is to give? What you give multiplies seven-fold back to you. Let us move on to another powerful insight.

CHAPTER 15

Giving: What It's All About

ONE OF THE GREATEST LAWS is the law of giving. It is a phenomenal law. Give freely and happily. Always form a habit of giving cheerfully. Give first, before you receive. Whatever energy you give will come back to you in an amazing way. You may give away your time, for example, and it comes back to you much later from an unexpected source in an unexpected form in a way that benefits you greatly. You cannot insist on a particular way and time for it to come back to you, but you can be assured it will come back in the best way for you. Give. Give. Give. And do so cheerfully and freely. It is the energy behind the giving that matters, so do not give grudgingly. The law of cause and effect guarantees that you shall receive plenty for what you give.

Life is for giving.

Give what you have—time, money, smiles, love, compliments, anything. And you will get back what you do not have.

—I am wealth. I am abundance. I am joy.—

Give graciously and receive gratefully. Grace and gratitude are the energizing factors of giving and receiving.

—I am wealth. I am abundance. I am joy.—

By taking care of society and nature, you take care of yourself. Share with and give to nature and society often. It is the goose that lays the golden eggs, and it needs to be protected and nourished so that it can protect and nourish you.

—I am wealth. I am abundance. I am joy.—

Share. Give. Help others. In the proportion and to the extent that you cause others to build their wealth, so will you build your own wealth.

—I am wealth. I am abundance. I am joy.—

Invest some money in financial services and institutions that lend money to others and enable others to build wealth. This is another great way for you to take care of society, to make it wealthy so that you may also get wealthier from it.

—I am wealth. I am abundance. I am joy.—

The universe is all energy. Energy flows. Giving promotes this energy flow, placing you in harmony with the powers of the universe. Whatever you wish to have, cause another being to have it first, and you will begin to have it in abundance. Give and you will receive in multiples. For example, if you wish to have wealth, show others how to have wealth, and in an amazing way, you will soon find yourself wealthy. It is a very complicated system that works perfectly. Give cheerfully!

—I am wealth. I am abundance. I am joy.—

Share, share, share. It is an investment banked with the universe that returns to you with amazing interest. Share gladly and genuinely.

—I am wealth. I am abundance. I am joy.—

What you wish to have, cause another to have. To have wealth and abundance, cause another to have it. How do you cause others to have wealth? Teach these lessons to your friends who are interested in wealth. Show them this book and others like it. Form study groups or mastermind circles with them. Where two or more are gathered, the whole is more than the sum of its parts.

—I am wealth. I am abundance. I am joy.—

Develop an awareness that enables you to look out for and see all opportunities where you can give something freely and cheerfully. You can give material things, your time, skills, or anything else.

—I am wealth. I am abundance. I am joy.—

Get out of the habit of thinking that you should receive something first, before you give. That is not giving. That is an exchange. Giving freely and cheerfully enables you to do business, if you wish to look at it that way, with the universe. This is how it works. You give someone something that you have now—freely and cheerfully. The universe, by law, finds the best way to give that energy back to you in the form of something that you do not have. It gives you back in multiples, when it is most appropriate, in the most appropriate form. It is a magical process. Obviously, the more you give, the more magic you create for yourself. Life starts to work for you.

—I am wealth. I am abundance. I am joy.—

Develop a strong desire and persistence to give cheerfully and freely.

—I am wealth. I am abundance. I am joy.—

In your goal-setting, remember to include several goals that are about free and cheerful giving. Giving, under the law of cause and effect, is one of the most powerful actions you can take. It returns in multiples, seven-fold. You cannot afford to leave out giving in your life plan. You cannot afford to leave it to chance occurrence.

—I am wealth. I am abundance. I am joy.—

Develop giving as a habit, something you do naturally without having to think of it. This makes you into a consistent and persistent giver, and the universe will work for you.

—I am wealth. I am abundance. I am joy.—

Give spontaneously.

—I am wealth. I am abundance. I am joy.—

Work on the habit of giving, until you get to the point where you enjoy giving. Enjoy it thoroughly.

—I am wealth. I am abundance. I am joy.—

It is okay to think and know that, when you give, you will get back something from the universe. You do not have to pretend you are not interested in receiving a reward for giving. Expecting reward is good. In fact, expecting a reward empowers that reward to come to you. You only violate the law of giving when you expect to receive something back from the same being you give to, saying: "Well, I did this for you so you should do that for me." In fact, demanding a particular reward back is a violation of the universal law. It focuses your mind on "trading" rather than on "cheerful and free giving." Never ask for or expect "payback" from those you give to. The reward you receive will come from a source and at a time and in a form that the universe finds best suited for you.

—I am wealth. I am abundance. I am joy.—

You always have something to give—time, compliments, talent, money, knowledge, sharing a book, etc.

—I am wealth. I am abundance. I am joy.—

Giving has one bonus effect: it shows you what you have but did not know you had. Say you wish to have wealth. You then decide to give wealth first by helping others learn how to have wealth. You read books like this one, help where you can with the knowledge you gain, share books and resources, and so on. In that process, magically, you end up realizing you had a whole lot of wealth and wealth capabilities that you previously thought you lacked.

—I am wealth. I am abundance. I am joy.—

You are surrounded with abundant opportunities to give, but you only see them when you decide to start seeing them.

—I am wealth. I am abundance. I am joy.—

Learn to receive graciously and happily as well. Do not feel uncomfortable receiving. You deserve it; and by receiving, you are in harmony with the law of giving and receiving.

—I am wealth. I am abundance. I am joy.—

The trick to giving is not to force it upon those you give to. Offer your gift freely and cheerfully. Show your hand. Do not shove. Show. If the recipient does not wish to take your gift, respect that cheerfully. Do not be offended if your gift is not accepted. Allow the other person full freedom of choice. And do not make a person dependent on you. When people become dependent on your gifts unnecessarily, you have not done them any good, because you have reduced their belief in themselves and their abilities.

—I am wealth. I am abundance. I am joy.—

Here is a likely scenario. Imagine a person who does not have much in material possessions to give and share with others. But this person is very charming and kind, and gives many compliments to people he or she comes across without even getting one compliment back. This person uplifts other people's mood and confidence by finding ways to encourage and compliment them, but never gets a compliment back from anybody. Well, not to worry. The universe keeps its accounts perfectly. This kind of giving builds credit in the universal system. One day, by the law of cause and effect, of giving and receiving, this person somehow gets the bicycle he or she has always wanted— just when it was needed—in a way that looks like a miracle. It could be by winning a competition or as a gift from a stranger, or one of countless other possibilities (what people call luck). That is how giving works. Sometimes the universe takes little things that you have, can give, and do give, and it puts them into one big thing that you do not have and require, and it gives that to you at a perfect time.

—I am wealth. I am abundance. I am joy.—

You give but little when you give of your possessions.
It is when you give of yourself that you truly give. For
what are possessions but things you keep and guard for
fear you may need them tomorrow? ...And what is fear
of need but fear itself? Is not dread of thirst when your
well is full, the thirst that is unquenchable? There are
those who give little of the much of which they have—
and they give it for recognition and their hidden desire

makes their gift unwholesome. And there are those who have little and give it all. These are the believers in life and the bounty of life, and their coffer is never empty... It is well to give when asked, but it is better to give unasked, through understanding... For in truth it is life that gives unto life—while you, who deem yourself a giver, are but a witness... and you are all receivers.

—*Kahlil Gibran, The Prophet*

—I am wealth. I am abundance. I am joy.—

All other things held constant, to the extent that an individual or society shares and gives in the right way, so will it have wealth and happiness.

Now you know how to do business with the universe, so to speak. The universe itself is a giving universe, for life is for giving. You give and you receive seven-fold—you actually are rewarded for your kindness. The Source, life, is all about giving; and the intelligence that runs the universe honors your giving always, all ways. Give cheerfully! Everything in life is a gift. Especially with regard to wealth and happiness, never cease to cause others to have wealth and happiness, and you will have wealth and happiness in multiples!

But what goes with giving? Receiving. And what goes with that? Gratitude, thank you! Let's have a look at gratitude.

CHAPTER 16
Gratitude: Sealing the Deal

A LL OF LIFE IS A GIFT. Every person, moment, and thing is a gift; it is only that we refuse to open the gifts, and hence we do not get the gift sent to us. All things come to those who are grateful. There is great truth to that, and here is why it works so well. By the law of cause and effect, your gratitude attracts that which you are grateful for. And you should be grateful even before you receive something because, by law, you know you will receive it. In fact, you have it even before you ask. Gratitude speeds that reception, because it is a statement of belief; you are already enthusiastically and genuinely grateful, in a state of gratitude, because of what you will receive, or more accurately, have received and are about to experience. Note—the gratitude is there before you even "receive" what you are seeking. In reality, you have it all already; you just are not experiencing it yet.

So gratitude is the first step to receiving and experiencing. It is an affirmation that you know you will have it. Imagine being grateful and getting excited about a future event—do you have any idea how much faith that portrays and how much that takes you toward your goals at rapid speed? It is magical! Gratitude creates and grows your faith, in addition to being the right thing to do.

Give thanks.

What you are grateful for reveals its gifts and serves you. Be grateful for everything because everything helps you discover an aspect of yourself.

—I am wealth. I am abundance. I am joy.—

The trick is to learn to accept everything that you have already, to love the present moment, all of it, and to prefer nothing but Now when you are in it. Doing this places you in a state of calmness and in a position most suitable for finding the gifts contained in the present moment, so that you can rapidly grow in the direction in which you wish to move.

—I am wealth. I am abundance. I am joy.—

Gratitude for all things in the past, present, and future works wonders.

—I am wealth. I am abundance. I am joy.—

All other things held constant, to the extent that an individual or society is grateful for everything and for each other, so will it have wealth and happiness.

Gratitude does not need much explanation—you already know how to be grateful. Inside of you, you know how magical it is. All you now need to recognize is that every moment, person, and thing was brought to you by your own choices, thoughts, actions, and states of being. You did it. The world just creates itself around you so that you may experience your Self and recreate yourself. So be grateful for every moment, thing, and person; this is the best way to find yourself. Remember, what you resist persists. Gratitude negates resistance. Once you are grateful, you can look at everything clearly and see yourself.

Another bonus of gratitude is faith. By being grateful now for things you intend to experience in the future, you become ever more certain that you will experience them, and this in turn brings them to you. It allows you to be excited about the future!

CHAPTER 17

Consciousness: You Experience What You Are Awake To

THIS BOOK HAS BEEN LARGELY ABOUT wealth consciousness. But what is consciousness? It is being awake to something. Wealth consciousness is being awake to wealth. Wealth has always been there, of course, but you may not have been awake to it. You cannot experience what you are unaware of. Consciousness is the set of attributes and capabilities that enable you to be awake to a state of being or a set of experiences. This book has been about the things that enable you to be awake to the wealth that is already there. And the happiness that is already there as well. So, my friend, wake up!

The material wealth of a nation is simply the manifestation of the collective wealth consciousness of that nation. That applies to any group of people—from families to corporations to continents to worlds. The least conscious person in a group of people will bring down the experiences of the most conscious. So wise people do whatever they can to raise the consciousness of the group at large so that they themselves may experience more. It is self-defeating to do nothing or to lower someone else's wealth consciousness.

—I am wealth. I am abundance. I am joy.—

Several studies show that many people who win over $1 million in lotteries end up worse off financially than they were before they won. They lose all that money in amazingly short periods and end up even worse off because of the new debts and liabilities they accumulate. It is not money that makes a person wealthy. It is wealth consciousness. People without wealth consciousness are unable to become wealthy, even when a huge sum of money comes their way in a lottery win. On the other hand, people with wealth consciousness cannot fail to have money and wealth for extended periods. They may go broke occasionally due to an error in thinking or a higher choice, but they always bounce back up. They have no fear of going broke because they know that, even if it happens, it is temporary, and they are designed to come right back up. You can take away all their money and, within a year, they will be wealthy again, or at least be on their way to wealth. Luck has nothing to do with it.

—I am wealth. I am abundance. I am joy.—

The greatest creative forces become available when your conscious, subconscious, and super-conscious selves are in harmony in their choices. You make them so by raising your consciousness and awareness to all three levels of your Self. You become aware and conscious of things you used to do subconsciously. You can do this by deciding to be aware. Decide to be mindful and deliberate; watch your thoughts and actions and dreams, instead of walking about daydreaming in a daze and doing things automatically. It is also a good idea to consider Vipassana (mindfulness) meditation. It is one of the best ways to increase your awareness.

You see, your Self makes choices, but if you are not aware of them, you will not know what they are. These choices are super-conscious. You start becoming aware of them by honoring your feelings (not emotions or thoughts masquerading as feelings, but genuine feelings). You also become aware of your super-conscious mind through meditation.

You make some choices consciously and you make some subconsciously. You can increase your awareness of your subconscious choices by deciding to be aware, by watching your thoughts. For example, in the past you may have had idle thoughts of fear and indecision regarding a particular topic. These thoughts went on in your head all the time as you did other things; they were background thoughts. Well, now what you should do is watch your thoughts and do not allow any idle daydreams that keep tossing about an issue like a wild monkey in a cage.

The point is that, if for a particular decision these three levels all choose differently, your results will obviously be mixed and confusing to you. The way to fix that is to raise your awareness on all levels.

—I am wealth. I am abundance. I am joy.—

The Source of all creation is a field of infinite possibilities and creativity. Our true Selves are one with the Source, in the same image and likeness. When we are conscious of that and believe it is so, we tap into this field of infinite possibilities and our inherent creative abilities.

—I am wealth. I am abundance. I am joy.—

You must have wealth consciousness that knows no poverty (or, more accurately, the illusion of poverty). Work on it until the idea of poverty is laughable—until to think that you can possibly become poor is a ridiculous idea to you.

—I am wealth. I am abundance. I am joy.—

You create money by increasing your value inside yourself. You do that by reading books like this. You also do that by remembering your true Self that is in the image and likeness of the Source—abundant by nature. You then experience money by exchanging the value you have built in you. Exchange it with others by providing services, goods, and money to others in exchange for their services, goods, and money. Remember that people have a unique purpose or ability within them. They fulfill part or all of this ability or purpose; they create something out of and by it by using their internal value. Their creations are therefore unique, and the exchange of these unique creations is what brings about paper money, or cash. Paper money is just a medium of exchange for our uniquely developed internal value. Build wealth by building your inner value. Experience wealth by carrying out your purpose and ability using that built-up inner value. It all lies inside you. To build external wealth, build internal value and then exercise it. It is that simple. The biggest components of internal value are instantly available to all. These are faith or certainty, imagination, inquiry, and focus. Activity, taking action, translates inner value into outer value, material wealth.

—I am wealth. I am abundance. I am joy.—

Wealth follows those with wealth consciousness, not the other way around. Wealth consciousness comes from states and thoughts of prosperity and wealth that are full of confidence. It does not allow any thoughts about poverty or limitations, doubt or scarcity. It does not allow states of fear and disbelief.

—I am wealth. I am abundance. I am joy.—

The earning of money has nothing to do with the direct manipulation of the paper you now call money. It has everything to do with wealth consciousness.

—I am wealth. I am abundance. I am joy.—

Wealth is a predictable result. The causes of wealth are predictable and accessible to all without exception.

—I am wealth. I am abundance. I am joy.—

To the extent that you have wealth consciousness inside of you, outside things will enable you to experience wealth or hinder you from experiencing it. This is the same for happiness. To the extent that you have happiness inside of you, outside things will enable you to experience happiness or hinder you from experiencing it. And it is the same for everything else—peace, love, non-judgment, non-condemnation, non-segregation, and so on.

—I am wealth. I am abundance. I am joy.—

The collective consciousness is very influential for your own wealth and happiness. You create many of the events in your life. But some events, especially the large ones, happen because of the thoughts and consciousness of people around you in your society and world. You have heard this before in many forms (where two or more are gathered…). You are not alone; you are not separate from everyone else. You, as an individual, matter a lot to the whole, and vice versa. Your extent of wealth and happiness is co-determined by yourself and everyone else. Please understand this carefully. No one can stop you from being happy and wealthy, because you alone choose to experience everything as good or bad all on your own, and no one can possibly take away that internal choice from you. And only you can choose to have wealth or happiness, and no one can take that from you except yourself.

That said, you are more likely to meet good and happy opportunities and events if the people around you are of a suitable consciousness. Think of your mind as an extension of your spirit, your body as an extension of your mind, your immediate environment and other people as an extension of your body, the world as an extension of your environment, and thus the whole world as your own larger extended body. And the same goes for everyone. Thus, whatever "good" or "bad" there is in your extended body affects you to the degree that it is "away" from you. So it is very much in your interests to spread wealth and happiness consciousness around the world to "improve" the larger extended body as a whole, for what happens to one part of the body affects the whole. The advancement of just one individual in society causes a series of advancements of varying degrees for all others in society. So to raise yourself, raise others—and you will automatically rise as well. Even telling a few people is enough, but telling as many as you can shifts this universe dramatically. This book is a start; share it. Use the Internet, e-mail, and text messaging on your mobile phone. We have invented these affordable communication networks as a testimony to our increasing realization that we are one and as a tool to keep growing in that realization. So use these networks; remember them.

—I am wealth. I am abundance. I am joy.—

One of the best ways to become wealthy and happy is by practicing meditation every day. Meditation puts you in touch with your higher self, so that the teachings in this book can become you, experientially, in every cell of your body. They will no longer be theoretical constructs, for they become you. You will no longer have to struggle to practice and remember them, for they are you. Start meditating, and one day soon, you will have this happen to you. The recommended meditation technique here is Vipassana (mindfulness/insight) meditation.

—I am wealth. I am abundance. I am joy.—

All other things held constant, to the extent that an individual or society has and develops wealth, health, and happiness consciousness in itself and in those around it, so will it have wealth, health, and happiness.

Now it is time to go to a wider dimension. It is time to look at what has this consciousness—the Self, the builder of the universe, the builder that uses space and time as materials to create experiences.

CHAPTER 18

The Self: Architect of the Universe

I
T IS NOW TIME TO LOOK AT FIRST CAUSE, that from which everything arises. Know thyself—so has it been said throughout the ages.

Your Self, your spirit, or your soul, whatever you call it, is the real you. The rest of you is just a set of tools. Your personality and body and ego are just temporary tools of your Self, which always remains even after you drop everything else.

Your Self is First Cause of your entire world. Any state you find yourself in must be caused by Self. Your thoughts come from your Self. Your desires come from your Self. Can you think of anything in the world that does not arise from the spirit? Nothing can exist outside of spirit; nothing can exist outside of life. Even wealth has First Cause. Now you see why it is crucial to know what spirit is, so that you may know how to be more in touch and aware of First Cause in your life, so that you may create the experience of wealth and happiness in your life.

We have already touched on spirit many times before in this book, especially when we were referring to states of being. Now we shall look at two aspects of Self—the actual spirit side of you and the things you do here in life as a personality. We'll consider what is healthy for you and your Self—what helps you to have wealth and happiness.

You are First Cause.

People attract what they are, not what they want. They attract what they love and what they fear. They sustain what they judge and condemn. What they resist persists. What they accept and examine mindfully releases them. What they truly believe is what becomes real in their lives.

—I am wealth. I am abundance. I am joy.—

See good in everything. Look at the light, and you will never see the dark.

—I am wealth. I am abundance. I am joy.—

Change is the only constant in the universe. Everything changes at every moment. Life is all about change, and with change comes growth. You will one day leave even your own body. You can never truly own anything here on earth. Thinking that you own something results in that thing owning you. The thought of ownership causes resistance to change, resistance to the workings of the mighty universe in its infinitely intelligent fashion. The minute you start thinking you own something, it owns you. For you to enjoy and use prosperity and wealth wisely and fruitfully, you must replace the idea of ownership with the idea of temporary custodianship—having the use of something, keeping something, of taking care of something. This is what makes you ready to "go with the flow" without loss and suffering when the time comes for change to work its inevitable ways. So much suffering is caused by resistance to change. Resistance to change shows that you believe it is possible not to have something, to lose something; yet on a higher level, on the level of spirit, you have it all at all times.

—I am wealth. I am abundance. I am joy.—

What are you holding yourself back for? You have it all. You can experience any part of your Self that you choose, so long as you make the choice earnestly and with conviction. With faith, everything is possible. It is all yours anyway.

—I am wealth. I am abundance. I am joy.—

What are you waiting for?

—I am wealth. I am abundance. I am joy.—

Calmness is the fruit of wisdom acquired over time. Calmness affords true control and precision of thought.

—I am wealth. I am abundance. I am joy.—

Celebrate life!

—I am wealth. I am abundance. I am joy.—

Fear of the unknown is paralyzing and totally unnecessary. Only in the unknown can you find growth, freshness, and creation. The known, the past, is already experienced—it is gone. A past moment is a moment gone, lingering only in your memory. Sometimes we keep recreating the past, over and over, sustaining it out of fear of losing it. But new growth, new creation, lies only in the unknown. Learn to love and cherish the gift and power of the unknown. Choose this, and you will find yourself traveling on a wonderful journey of exploration and growth. Remember always that your Self knows everything—nothing is unknown to it. It is only your ego—with its limited perspective of space-time—that knows only fractions of the All. Trust your spirit—your Self can never harm you. You are your Self, not your body and ego. All suffering is caused by fear and by believing strongly in the illusions of this world. Let go.

—I am wealth. I am abundance. I am joy.—

The unknown carries tremendous opportunities, knowledge, potential, and rewards. Step into it often.

—I am wealth. I am abundance. I am joy.—

Consistency of purpose. Curiosity. Confidence. Courage. Cheer. Certainty of intention. This is all good stuff.

—I am wealth. I am abundance. I am joy.—

Why are you holding back?

—I am wealth. I am abundance. I am joy.—

Let go.

—I am wealth. I am abundance. I am joy.—

At every moment and in every situation, with every thought and action, ask yourself two questions:

Is this the greatest version of the grandest vision I have ever had of myself?

What would love do?

Then adjust your thoughts and actions based on the answers to these two questions. This is a very fast way to grow in all areas of your life.

—I am wealth. I am abundance. I am joy.—

Question everything and rule out nothing. Be willing to suspend everything you know. You cannot discover new things until you stop telling those new things what you think they should be. Let them tell you what they really are!

—I am wealth. I am abundance. I am joy.—

Exercise your body daily. Your body is an energy system and an extension of your mind. Exercising opens up the energy channels in your mind and body. Remember, thought is energy, and your mind is all over your body, in every cell of your body, not just in your brain. Exercising your body every day makes your mind and thoughts a great deal better.

—I am wealth. I am abundance. I am joy.—

Change is the only constant. Love it. Embrace it. Find the gifts that it brings to you. Change. It is the only game there is anyway—the game of life, the game of changes.

—I am wealth. I am abundance. I am joy.—

To the extent that a person has and exercises their wealth consciousness, that person finds themselves in the company of opportunities, businesses, situations, and people that enable them to manifest into physical form the amount of wealth consciousness they have and choose to exercise. Luck and coincidence have nothing to do with it. What some people call luck and coincidence is the precise execution of an infinitely intelligent universe that works in amazing ways to fulfill exactly what we imagine ourselves to be, with conviction.

—I am wealth. I am abundance. I am joy.—

You are your own luck.

—I am wealth. I am abundance. I am joy.—

What is "can"? What is "should"? What is the line between can and cannot, should and should not? Is there really such a line? Or do you, we, make it up?

—I am wealth. I am abundance. I am joy.—

You are the magic.

—I am wealth. I am abundance. I am joy.—

Change is the order of the universe. Life is change. Growth and evolution is what life is all about. Clinging to things is not only futile; it is harmful to you. You cannot win a game when you resist change.

—I am wealth. I am abundance. I am joy.—

Now that you know the truth, the laws that drive the universe unfailingly, hold this truth in your thoughts at all times and you will not be affected by the physical world again. You will become its master instead of its slave. The truth will set you free.

—I am wealth. I am abundance. I am joy.—

Life is all about growth, expansion of consciousness. Life, the Source, God, has never designed or planned that you should not expand your consciousness. In fact, the whole design of life is for consciousness to keep expanding. It is in the whole universe's best interests that you expand your consciousness, including your wealth consciousness. Life seeks to express and experience itself to enable that evolution and growth. Wealth, if you consider it clearly, does a whole lot to enable that growth. Once you have wealth, you have freedom to explore many other aspects of life you would not have had a chance to explore without it. The true nature of all life is to increase life. Anything to the contrary is going against life. Your desire for wealth is very natural and necessary for you to move on to higher levels. Not only is it natural, it is fully supported by nature if only you follow the laws of nature. Ancient texts tell us that it is the desire of God that you get rich, and nature is friendly to your plans, as long as you are in harmony with it.

—I am wealth. I am abundance. I am joy.—

We live in a realm of relativity. Everything else outside of you exists, in a most clever way, to help you know yourself and recreate yourself anew. It is most clever, because that statement is true for each being. Without short people, tall people would never know they were tall. Without "bad" people, "good" people would never know they were "good." And vice versa. You need a frame of reference and an opposite to know what you are, and to choose what to become next. The day you start seeing everyone and everything as bringers of certain gifts for you—when you seek to find out what those gifts are and you realize you are also there to enable the self-definition of others and willingly give others what they ask—that is the day you will start moving very rapidly toward more wealth.

—I am wealth. I am abundance. I am joy.—

Love yourself, your customers, your world, your family, everyone and everything. Love is the strongest power.

—I am wealth. I am abundance. I am joy.—

So you wish to be wealthy. That is great. But who are you? That is a very deep question. Ask yourself: "Who am I?" Your first answer may be "I am Jane" or "I am Joe." Then you may say something like, "I am a twenty-eight-year old female, Croatian, short-tempered but happy, sometimes doubtful but generally confident." Really? Is that really you? Each of those things started at some point in time. Your parents gave you a name; you acquired your habits, personality, and disposition over time. You were born with few of these things, and you were conceived with none of them. In other words, none of these things is really you—you leave them all here on this plane of existence when you move on to the next plane. So they are not the real you, your Self. They are "jackets" you wear over your Self—jackets that you take off as time goes by (people change), and some that you take off when you leave the earth.

Try this: "I am a twenty-eight-year old female." Is your Self really only twenty-eight years old? Could it have been there before you were conceived into this world? Is your Self definitely male or female? You do not have to know the answers to these questions to become wealthy. But it is important to recognize that, just as we said and saw that you are not your circumstances, you are also not some of the things you have all along thought you were. These "jackets" are helpful and useful, but sometimes they can hold you back. People who identify too much with their jackets, especially negative ones, place themselves in a prison, a box, a position from which they are unable to escape for fear that their self will be violated, or that their self is not capable, while all along it isn't their true Self. The next time you catch yourself saying "I can't do that because I am..." reexamine the "I am" bit and ask yourself whether that is really you or a jacket you picked up along the way, a jacket that you know for sure you will one day take off, a jacket that you may as well take off now.

Your body cells change daily; your thoughts come and go; your ego and self-image change. They are not the real you. Your Self is the timeless Being that takes on all these jackets of illusion—jackets that should serve you, not hinder you—jackets that are really under your Self-control, although often you forget this. The illusions, the jackets, are very necessary. They are the tools by which your Self experiences itself on a physical plane. Think about what you know so far about spirit and quantum physics. All physical objects look separate to our limited five senses; but, in fact, they are part of a large pool of energy that is not separated at all. Spirit is also just One, individuated into "individual people." It is individuated, not separated—just as the oceans of the world are individuated into waters with different depths and tides and characteristics, yet they are all one ocean. All your spirit knows is love, for it cannot kill or injure itself—it is immortal. It is also One. It cannot "go broke," for it has everything, pure wealth and abundance.

Why is it necessary for the spirit to have an earthly existence? Imagine that you were born in a very rich land where everyone was super wealthy, no one lacked anything, and all desires were fulfilled instantly. How would you ever experience the thrill of having wealth? It would be impossible. You would know you were wealthy, but this would be meaningless because you would never have compared it with being poor. You would never have risen out of poverty and become wealthy. See? You would need first to "go broke" in this super wealthy land, then appreciate how uncomfortable that felt, then work your way back to wealth to feel the thrill and experience of wealth.

You cannot experience something, even if you know it, unless you create the experience of its opposite. This is the position spirit is in; it knows all, but it cannot experience wealth unless it creates a realm of illusion of not knowing and not having. Let us go back to our example. If everything in that super wealthy land were wealth, you would be unable to become poor. So you would have to create an illusion where you saw only extremely small segments of your whole world at a time. For instance, instead of seeing that you have a car, a road, a house, and a shopping mall all at once, the illusion would limit your vision so you can only see the car—at first. Then, after working, you would start seeing the house. And so on. Once you could see it all, you would feel the thrill of realizing what you already knew and had all along but could not experience. This is the purpose of our earthly physical experience.

Another way to look at it is to think of something you really like. Think of your favorite food or even having great sex with your loved one. If you ate your favorite food all the time, at every moment of your waking and sleeping, or if you did the same with sex, do you see how the experience would cease to be an experience and become a knowing without experience, for it would be all that is. Your entire eating experience would be comprised of eating that one favorite food, and you would finally know no other eating experience, and the favorite food would cease to thrill. This is a very simple example; it gets very complicated at the highest spiritual level, but at least you get the picture.

Still not convinced? Here is another example—the experience of love. Spirit is immortal and at one with all. It knows only love, but cannot experience it because there is nothing to compare it to. At the ultimate level of spirit, all that exists is One and the One knows that it is all One; it has no illusions of separation. This is what some people call God. Let us think of it as Being, life, or the Source, the All That Is, the I Am. All That Is, life, Being, is exactly that—all. It is not a he or she or an it—it is All. There is nothing else except the One, so there is nothing the One can use to experience itself unless it individuates itself. The individuation and illusions start at lower levels. It is necessary to create a limited-consciousness physical plane where the illusion of separation exists, where it is possible to "kill" a body, to hurt, to suffer, to lack. And on this physical plane—where it is possible to act in unloving ways and do harm—love rises, and its fruits and the experience of it are then possible.

Now you see that the illusion is very necessary. You, your Self, need it and use it. The only problem comes when your ego makes you believe in the illusion. The ego was designed to create the illusion of separation. It is necessary. But when the illusion is taken as the reality, it no longer becomes a tool with which you can experience the greatness of your spirit and all that it has. It instead becomes a painful trap. You stop "pretending" that you do not have wealth in order to experience the thrill of having wealth, and instead start "believing" that you really do not have wealth. You stop pretending that you are separate and at risk, and start believing that you are. This is the cause of much suffering. Learn to use the illusion instead of believing in it. This is what Jesus meant when he said: "Be in this world but not of it."

Simply being aware of who you really are will change your life amazingly for the positive. You are a spirit with a body, personality, and ego. You are not a body, personality, and ego with a spirit.

—I am wealth. I am abundance. I am joy.—

The most important thing is definitely to have joy in your life. Lighten up; do not take things so seriously; do not be too hard on yourself and others; let joy into the lives of people. Joy is natural; it is the soul expressing itself. It keeps the energy circulating and makes the whole ride worth it! Joy multiplies everything it attracts. And it is fun. Enjoy!

Decide at all times not to worry, not to get frustrated, not to wish you were somewhere else doing something else, and not to fear. All these are statements of *not having*, and they perpetuate the state of *not having*.

—I am wealth. I am abundance. I am joy.—

Before you do anything, always ask yourself: "Is this who I Am?" "Is this how I wish to define myself into a higher next?"

—I am wealth. I am abundance. I am joy.—

It is all inside of you.

—I am wealth. I am abundance. I am joy.—

For everything you see around you, you are the cause. Why then would you hate something around you now? If you don't wish to have it around anymore, ask yourself what part or aspect of yourself is causing it, and you will soon discover something about yourself that you will find beneficial to change.

—I am wealth. I am abundance. I am joy.—

Nothing happens around you of which you are not wholly or partly a cause at some level of your whole Self, even though you may not be conscious of the choices you are making that are causing your world.

—I am wealth. I am abundance. I am joy.—

Condemnation and judgment keep in place that which is condemned and judged.

—I am wealth. I am abundance. I am joy.—

You are not your past, any of it, at all, unless you insist you are.

—I am wealth. I am abundance. I am joy.—

Your soul is the part of you closest to the Source of All That Is. It is an individuation of the Source, in the image and likeness of the Source. Your soul knows and perceives a lot more than your physical body and mind do. Your soul communicates with your mind through your body using feelings and intuition. Listen to your feelings and intuition always if you wish to speed up your growth and reduce unnecessary setbacks and suffering.

—I am wealth. I am abundance. I am joy.—

You are a soul with a body, not a body with a soul. You are a soul with a body, a mind, a personality, and an ego. Knowing this and knowing what a soul is makes a huge and empowering difference in the acquisition of wealth.

—I am wealth. I am abundance. I am joy.—

Meditation places you in direct contact with the unified field of consciousness, the unified mind, and infinite intelligence. Through meditation, a completely new world will open up to you. Through meditation, you will find calmness, wisdom, and inspiration. It is yet another way toward wealth and many other things. It is the home of infinite wealth consciousness, and you are welcome to it any time.

—I am wealth. I am abundance. I am joy.—

Inspiration and desire come from the soul seeking expression and manifestation in the physical world. One fast track to get to where you are going is to pay attention to your desires and inspirations. Develop your intuition.

—I am wealth. I am abundance. I am joy.—

Mind, body, and spirit are all connected. One way to think of it is to see the mind as the subtlest part of the body, and the body as the most solid part of the mind. By living in this knowledge—by treating mind, body, and spirit with equal importance, care, and attention— you grow most quickly and become wealthy fastest.

—I am wealth. I am abundance. I am joy.—

The root of a bulb which shall produce a white lily is an unsightly thing; one might look upon it with disgust. But how foolish we should be to condemn the bulb for its appearance when we know the lily is within it. The root is perfect after its kind; it is a perfect but incomplete lily, and so we must learn to look upon every man and woman, no matter how unlovely in outward manifestation; they are perfect in their stage of being and they are becoming complete. Behold, it is all very good… It will make an immense difference with your faith and spirit whether you look upon civilization as a good thing which is becoming better or as a bad and evil thing which is decaying. One viewpoint gives you an advancing and expanding mind and the other gives you a descending and decreasing mind. One viewpoint will make you grow greater and the other will inevitably cause you to grow smaller. One will enable you to work for the eternal things; to do large works in a great way toward the completing of all that is incomplete and in-harmonious; and the other will make you a mere patch-work reformer, working almost without hope to save a few lost souls from what you will grow to consider a lost and doomed world. So you see it makes a vast difference to you, this matter of the social viewpoint. "All's right with the world. Nothing can possibly be wrong but my personal attitude, and I will make that right. I will see the facts of nature and all the events, circumstances, and conditions of society, politics, government, and indus-try from the highest viewpoint. It is all perfect, though incomplete. It is all the handiwork of God; behold, it is all very good."

—*James Allen*

—I am wealth. I am abundance. I am joy.—

How do you start doing all these things? Just start doing them. Now. It is that simple. Just do it. Now.

—I am wealth. I am abundance. I am joy.—

Your truth is always truest to you. Truth is personal and ever-changing. Even though you should surround yourself with experts, advisors, and good books, always follow what rings true to you. Do not follow external sources blindly; check them with your Self.

—I am wealth. I am abundance. I am joy.—

The Source always talks to all of us through all forms of internal and external communication. Always in all ways. It is we who shut out that communication. Start paying attention to the movies you watch, the TV shows you see, the magazines you read, the people you talk to, the events of life that you watch, and the intuitions you have. All these, and many more, carry messages for your advancement, messages from the Source. Simply be open and willing.

—I am wealth. I am abundance. I am joy.—

Act as if you are already wealthy, for you are.

—I am wealth. I am abundance. I am joy.—

There are no real limits other than those you set on yourself.

—I am wealth. I am abundance. I am joy.—

Become unstoppable by refusing to stop.

—I am wealth. I am abundance. I am joy.—

It's a little like wrestling a gorilla. You don't quit when you're tired, you quit when the gorilla is tired.

—Robert Strauss

—I am wealth. I am abundance. I am joy.—

You have more potential in you than you can possibly use up in an entire lifetime or even in several lifetimes. Stop making up excuses and believing in limits.

—I am wealth. I am abundance. I am joy.—

By our inherent nature, we have limitless potential and abilities. "I can't" does not exist—it is an illusion. If nothing outside yourself can hold you back, then what *is* holding you back?

—I am wealth. I am abundance. I am joy.—

Your soul is that part of you that is closest to God, the Source. Your soul speaks to your mind through feelings and intuition. Listen to your feelings and intuition. Honor them over any conflicting thoughts and emotions. Be careful, though, because some thoughts and emotions camouflage themselves as feelings. But be still and you can distinguish between them.

—I am wealth. I am abundance. I am joy.—

The desires that you suppress become depressions, and that leads to something even worse. It can sometimes lead to unhealthy ways to fulfill those suppressed desires. Express your desires, and you create life and joy.

—I am wealth. I am abundance. I am joy.—

Persist in following your feelings and intuition. They are your closest communications with the Source.

—I am wealth. I am abundance. I am joy.—

You are a soul with a body, not a body with a soul. When you see this clearly and live your life at all times with this in mind, your power increases.

—I am wealth. I am abundance. I am joy.—

"I Am." This is your new way of making statements. "I Am." The universe absolutely listens to whatever you place after the phrase "I Am."

—I am wealth. I am abundance. I am joy.—

You need nothing outside of yourself to be wealthy.

—I am wealth. I am abundance. I am joy.—

Freedom. It is your nature. Keep it and express it. Allow others to keep and express their freedom.

—I am wealth. I am abundance. I am joy.—

Stop choosing what has been chosen for you by others and start choosing on your own.

—I am wealth. I am abundance. I am joy.—

Meditate every day, even for just fifteen minutes twice a day. This connects you with the Source, lets you know your true nature, brings inspiration, and shows you the ultimate reality.

—I am wealth. I am abundance. I am joy.—

You are who you say you are.

—I am wealth. I am abundance. I am joy.—

Experiences are within you, not outside. For example, two people can take the same roller-coaster ride in an amusement park. One walks out of that ride very happy and thrilled, and the effects of that, over a lifetime, are positive, for everything is a cause of something else. The other person walks out of that same ride full of fear and shock, and the effects of that, over a lifetime, are negative. The same ride was experienced in two very different ways by two people. No experience exists outside of the person experiencing it. Even what you may consider a terrible event is joyous to someone somewhere. The point is that, when you choose to experience things positively, your life will be positive. The meaning of everything is the meaning you give it, and your experiences are what you say they are.

—I am wealth. I am abundance. I am joy.—

The next time a situation comes up, see it as the illusion it is; decide the experience you will have of it; then recreate yourself anew so that the illusion changes to your liking. This is so for financial situations and all other situations in life.

—I am wealth. I am abundance. I am joy.—

A healthy person is usually in a better position to create wealth. Health is an indication of agreement between your body, mind, and spirit. Lack of health is caused by a disagreement between these three: for example, a mind with negative thoughts and anger causes an unhealthy body. A body that is not rested, nourished, exercised, and kept free of toxins kills the mind. Listen to, notice, and honor what signs your body, mind, and spirit give you.

—I am wealth. I am abundance. I am joy.—

A daily combination of exercise and meditation raises your energy levels and positive emotions, leaving you in an extremely powerful position to create wealth and growth.

—I am wealth. I am abundance. I am joy.—

Remember "I Am." The universe, the Source, manifests to perfection all your "I Am" statements and states of being made with certainty. The only time in the universe is Now—the present time. "I Am" works and is in agreement with the ever-present time of Now by being in the present tense. "I will be" barely makes it.

—I am wealth. I am abundance. I am joy.—

Freedom. Maintain yours and allow others theirs.

—I am wealth. I am abundance. I am joy.—

Do not take life too seriously. Enjoy it! Play with it like a child. Laugh at every corner. Joy is your true nature, and aligning with your true nature boosts your acquisition of wealth.

—I am wealth. I am abundance. I am joy.—

Rest and eat properly. Recharge your mind and body's energy system.

—I am wealth. I am abundance. I am joy.—

You become more conscious of your unconscious aspects by raising your awareness. You do this by deciding to be aware of all your thoughts and actions. Be watchful and guide them. You enhance this greatly by meditation. A good technique is the Vipassana (insight) mindfulness meditation.

—I am wealth. I am abundance. I am joy.—

Here is an amazing truth. As you enrich your inner self with enlightenments, your outer self will grow correspondingly richer, yet you will become more and more indifferent to riches, and riches will let go of their obsessive hold on you. You will finally become a naturally and automatically wealthy person with the carefree abandon of a child, and you will enjoy freely.

—I am wealth. I am abundance. I am joy.—

Desires indicate to you things for which you have a built-in ability. You may never have piloted an airplane before, but if you have a desire to do so, it shows you that your Self has the ability and nature to learn to pilot a plane. In truth, your Self knows all there is to know, but a desire shows you that you, at the higher level of your soul, are fully supporting that desire to pilot planes, and the whole universe will be there to assist in that desire manifesting. It is advisable for a person to follow their desires in business as well; in this way, you have proof that you will be able to do what you desire, and you will enjoy it. Desires also indicate to you which parts of your Self are calling out for attention, evolution, and growth, and which are working out to perfection. Desires are signals from the Self.

—I am wealth. I am abundance. I am joy.—

Let us revisit time. You now know what time is. It is an illusion created by your consciousness seeing only small portions of the whole space-time continuum at once. Remember the example of the football field. You saw that an object on that field sees events taking time as it moves across the field from one event to another, but the field itself sees all events as taking place on it simultaneously. For the field, there is no time, only an ever-present moment of Now whereby all events (all objects on the field) are taking place at the same time.

Your consciousness is an object on that field. So what is the field? It is your spirit or soul. You may have imagined that your spirit is the same size as your consciousness, but in fact, it is much larger than that. It covers all aspects of your life, even those to which you are not awake, those you are not conscious of. It exists right now in your past and future, but you are only awake to the part of it that is in your present. Your spirit is eternal and its presence is timeless, but your consciousness is not. It is multi-dimensional, while your consciousness is usually four-dimensional.

The point here is this: your spirit communicates to you through intuition and feelings. It knows your future, and all possible combinations of it. But it needs your consciousness to experience what it knows. In fact, it knows everything, but it needs consciousness on a physical plane to experience what it knows conceptually. Your Self knows exactly what time each event in your future will take place, and exactly what you need now to make it take place then. But your future is not fixed. It changes with every choice you make. And whatever choice you make, your spirit knows the series of events after that. And if you wish to get to a certain point in your life in the future, it knows how to get there exactly, step by step.

There is an old saying that says, "When spirit commands, the universe obeys." To the spirit, everything is instantaneous, for it is all over the "field" at the same time. A big reason why you experience non-instantaneous gratification of your wishes is that you may not be listening to the spirit. The main reason that things seem to take time to manifest into experience after you wish them to be is that you may not be listening to the spirit. If you are aware of what the spirit is choosing at every stage and you know this through intuition and feelings, you will choose the same; and as soon as you choose, you will find that what you chose has popped up right in your face, ready to be experienced.

Try to see this. Your spirit has everything instantaneously. There are no delays between choice and having. But your consciousness usually experiences a delay. That delay is caused by differences between what your ego—your personality here on earth—chooses and what your Self chooses. Remember, you are your Self, but you also have an ego and personality and mind. So all choices are yours, but your spirit's choices are the most powerful, so to speak. Yet all choices are acted upon by the universe. If your Self chooses to experience a choice called A1 and your ego chooses A2, you will get to A2, but you will experience a "delay" in "time" due to the "confusion" of both choices being passed on to the universe. But if your ego and your spirit both choose A1, then you will find no delay at all. People now call these occurrences *synchronicity*. Synchronicity happens when you think of something or someone, and the same thing or person immediately, "coincidentally," appears or calls you. And you say, "Wow! What a coincidence!" But it is not a coincidence; it is just unison between spirit choices and ego choices, between mind and emotional choices. When all your other parts choose what your spirit chooses, the result of the choice is instantaneous.

You see, your desires arise from the spirit. Spirit chooses just the right sequence of events to arrive at a desired end. Remember, you are your spirit, so these are your choices. But you have many components and levels, some of which you are not conscious of unless you choose to be. Fear is in the world of ego. So are emotions and non-detachment. These things inhibit instantaneous manifestation of your choices, even if you know what spirit is choosing. And fear is false evidence appearing real. Emotions are past conditioning; they are reactions instead of creation, and life is about creation. Non-detachment rises out of fear, out of illusion that loss and failure are actual.

Learn to be aware, intuitive, detached, and creative instead of reactive. Start seeing fear as false evidence appearing real, and you will start to experience more and more of your choices the instant you make them or very soon after you make them. Learn to trust your intuition. Realize that you are a soul, and that your true nature is indestructible and all knowing, literally located everywhere—and you have it all. Your body and ego are just illusions made to enable you to experience your Self. You, at the level of spirit, are in your future even right now as you read this. Why then would you fear the next moment? It is already taken care of by you—and you cannot possibly hurt yourself. Even death, the thing that people fear most, is senseless to fear.

Think about it. If the spirit is done with its body, what can the body possibly do to prevent the spirit from leaving and taking away life? Nothing! If your spirit chooses to move on, that is it. It cannot be "trapped." And what can the body do to leave the spirit if the spirit still needs the body? Nothing! Your spirit is in past, present, and future and can see things that your body cannot. Your body cannot conspire against your spirit. Do you see how ego fights a fruitless war of fear against death and everything else? Do you see how fear itself is the destroyer? Spirit loses nothing. It cannot possibly lose. Spirit knows that, even after the body dies (changes form), it is still intact and as it was before, and it is all good. It is ego that fears death, and only because death is unknown. People who know death cease to fear it, as you may have heard.

Now, think about your birth. Just as you may not be aware of all the choices you are making as spirit, you most likely are unaware of the choices you made with regard to your birth. That does not mean there were no choices made, however. You chose a purpose, as we saw in the chapter on purpose. You had many purposes, desires, and wishes for further growth in various aspects. You chose exactly the right circumstances, body, configuration, and location to be born in to fulfill your desires, purposes, and choices for growth, and to stop believing in certain illusions. At every moment, you sent yourself the right people and things in your life to take you to the next step. Sometimes your ego refused to take them, but nevertheless you sent them. Do you start to see how it all works?

If you are still not convinced, think about this. Why do people say, when they are thinking of suicide: "I can't live with myself any more"? Look at that statement. There are two people in it. It is like a person saying: "I cannot live with this other guy anymore." Yet it is two "individuals" in one. One of them feels immortal and desires to end association with the other, which it knows is mortal and the source of suffering. Deep within everybody, there is knowledge that we are immortal souls with mortal, illusionary bodies and egos. All suffering comes from believing that our illusionary part is the real part. It is when we live in the illusion, instead of using it as we are here to do, that we cause pain and lack. The illusions are very necessary; they are beautiful gifts. But start using them instead of living in them.

—I am wealth. I am abundance. I am joy.—

Vipassana (insight or mindfulness) meditation takes your awareness to a level where you can watch your subconscious mind create thought. You can observe your sponsoring thoughts. It gives you a chance to "fix" your subconscious and ego through a process called mindfulness. It also takes you to levels beyond the subconscious. It is a wonderful tool.

—I am wealth. I am abundance. I am joy.—

You are your spirit, not your body, personality, conditions, or anything else. Your spirit is eternal and All That Is. Your spirit is real, you are spirit. You are real. The real creates the illusion, not the other way around.

—I am wealth. I am abundance. I am joy.—

The spirit or soul chooses a purpose or purposes when it chooses to manifest itself as a human being on earth. This purpose is co-chosen with all other spirits, with the One. It chooses what it wishes to experience on this physical plane. It causes a body and mind to experience these things. Now, it communicates to the body and mind through desires and feelings. But it never enforces its choices. Body and mind are free to choose whether or not to experience those desires. Often, out of fear or past conditioning, they choose not to. Yet the desire does not go away; it remains until it is fulfilled. When the body and mind are in disagreement or opposition to the soul, a person experiences dissatisfaction. When body, mind, and soul agree, the creative force is phenomenal—"waiting" ends, and joyous experience occurs without resistance. The soul then knows itself experientially! At all times, you are free to choose what you wish to experience. And at all times, your soul communicates to you, but you can choose not to listen, as many people have often done in the past.

—I am wealth. I am abundance. I am joy.—

Nothing real can be threatened.

—A Course in Miracles

—I am wealth. I am abundance. I am joy.—

All other things held constant, to the extent that an individual or society lives as a soul with a body, mind, and ego, instead of the other way around, so will it have wealth and happiness.

The greatest advice that can be given to you now is this: Meditate daily. If you do not go within, you go without. Meditation takes you in to meet your Self and infinity—One. It cannot be explained, only experienced.

Now let's take a brief look at the One.

CHAPTER 19

One: All That Is

INDUISM TAUGHT THESE LESSONS in a different way. Buddhism taught these lessons in a different way. Tao taught these lessons in a different way. Jesus and Mohammed both taught these lessons in a different way. Today, quantum physics teaches them in a different way. Just about every spiritual teacher, sage, quantum physicist, and religion teach, in their own way, that we are all one. By acting in that awareness, we move forward fastest, most richly, and least painfully. This is nothing new, but we have often refused to listen. Now, in your quest for wealth and joy, you may wish to look at this again.

Everything is One, the same Being, individuated in different guises. In other words, everything is a localized point in and of the Source, of the All That Is, of God. Nothing can possibly exist outside of and separate from the Source. The individuation and illusions of separation are necessary, as we saw in the chapter on Self. But they are only great tools when used as tools. When they are believed in as realities instead of as illusions, they destroy and cause unnecessary suffering and inadequacy.

Let us look, very briefly, into this Oneness. Once you realize, feel, and act from the position of Oneness, you will start seeing that you already are one with all the things you desire and with all the people and things that will bring wealth to you. You will see that you are simultaneously the one making the request, the one communicating the request, the one fulfilling the request, and the one experiencing the manifestation of the request. Hence, you need not worry. The illusion that you are not the same one doing all this is there just for your thrill and experience. This chapter will take a brief look at this Oneness, just to give you evidence for it and to start you thinking about it. It will merely start you on a journey that only you can take, for that journey cannot be described, only experienced. We are all One.

You are one with the Source, and nothing is difficult or denied from, by, and to the Source. The universe is friendly to your desires. Nothing is impossible, if only you believe.

—I am wealth. I am abundance. I am joy.—

You can never permanently own anything on earth. Life is change, and One is all there is. Ownership is a detrimental state of mind that allows what you think you own to own you. Again, here on earth, what you think you own ends up owning you, possessing you, taking away a part of your freedom. Think about that for a moment. Everything is One. How, then, can you own a part of the One? How can your hand own your leg? Your hand can play with your leg for a while, but it cannot own it. This works the same way with you and the rest of life. When you think you own something, you chase it about to prevent the loss of it, a chase that is fruitless. Hence, it owns you.

Instead, think of yourself as a custodian of things until it is time to relinquish them. Whether you like it or not, when the time comes or when your life on earth moves on, you will have to release all these things. Even your own body is eventually released from its present form. So enjoy, share, and have these things, but do not think that you are their owner. You can be something, but you cannot really own something. It is all One, and One is always changing.

—I am wealth. I am abundance. I am joy.—

Everything and everyone are connected. All life is one. What happens in Kabul affects you, somehow, wherever you are. And what happens with you, the thoughts you have and so on, affects everyone else everywhere, somehow. So for your own sake, think, act, and be as One.

—I am wealth. I am abundance. I am joy.—

Superiority and inferiority are not built into people and things. Seeing things in terms of better or worse is a judgmental weakness. This is especially a weakness of nations, whereby one government considers itself superior to another—especially in its economy or its governmental system. It is also a weakness of social classes. An extremely high number of wars, corporate collapses, and societal divides have been caused by the idea that "my way is better than your way." Disharmony is costly and never profitable in the long term for anybody. Harmony is extremely profitable. You can avoid disharmony by looking at everyone around you—not as better or worse compared to you or anything else—but as different. In other words, one entity's way is not a better or worse way; it is just a different way. This is a much more peaceful and profitable approach to everyone and everything else. Being special is not the same as being better. An entity can be special, but that does not make it better.

—I am wealth. I am abundance. I am joy.—

If you wish always to be in harmony with the incredibly powerful laws of the universe, simply act as if the whole universe is one unit with no separation between its seemingly separated components. For example, to know how to handle a business opponent in a way that will profit you the most, act as if your opponent and you are one. Treat him or her that way.

—I am wealth. I am abundance. I am joy.—

There is not a person alive who is not capable of greatly contributing to the well-being of this planet. Just changing your attitude can affect the world around you.

—*Susan Jeffers*

—I am wealth. I am abundance. I am joy.—

It is in your best interests to do your part to ensure that people all over the earth have wealth consciousness and joy. Many thinkers and scientists are beginning to show that an individual's thoughts affect the whole world's thoughts. An individual is responsible for what happens in the world and to everyone in it. The ancient Greeks had a similar concept—Gaia. This philosophy has been espoused by many thinkers all over the world—from Plato in ancient Greece, to Buddha in the Near and Far East. Modern scientists and thinkers in various fields of science are also starting to study and show that we are all connected. These connections are being found in various forms and in various fields of science by researchers including Dr. John Lovelock, Peter Russell (*The Global Brain Awakens*), British biologist Rupert Sheldrake (*A New Science of Life*), Howard Bloom (*Global Brain*), and many others. If you wish to be wealthy, you can do so on your own. But you can do so a lot more easily and to a much larger extent if you help the world attain wealth consciousness.

—I am wealth. I am abundance. I am joy.—

It has been said before in many places that the reason the One chooses to individuate Itself is this: In the absence of That Which Is Not, That Which Is, Is Not. Think about that.

—I am wealth. I am abundance. I am joy.—

So the wrong-doer cannot do wrong without the hidden will of you all… And when one of you falls down he falls for those behind him, a caution against the stumbling stone. Ay, and he falls for those ahead of him, who, though faster and surer of foot, yet removed not the stumbling stone… The murdered is not unaccountable for his own murder, and the robbed is not blameless for being robbed… Yea, the guilty is oftentimes the victim of the injured.

—Kahlil Gibran

—I am wealth. I am abundance. I am joy.—

Let us revisit quantum physics briefly. We saw that subatomic particles are what make up the physical universe. We also saw that these particles have intelligence. And we saw that this pure energy has intelligence. It also has remarkable properties, like being able to be in two places at once, to move from here to there without crossing the gap between, to travel back and forth in time, and so on. We also saw that we are in relation to and in collaboration with these particles, for what we choose to observe is what becomes, emerging out of this energy pool. Now, what do you suppose these energy packets are? What is pure energy?

Before we attempt to answer that question, let us look at the Source, All That Is, what many call God. We have been told that we are children of God, created in the image and likeness of God, and that God is All That Is. Now, let us go back to where God was the absolute Only, before "creation." In truth, there is no such linear time line, but let us imagine that there is, for the sake of study. On this time line, God was out there before creation, all alone. Remember, in the absence of That Which Is Not, That Which Is, Is Not. In the realm of the absolute, there exists only One with nothing else to compare Itself against. So for the One to experience Itself was not possible. To do this, the One had to individuate into a Duality, a realm of Relativity.

When the One did that, there now was a "this" and a "that"—a duality that could allow experience. We will call this the Initial Duality. Day could experience itself against night, and vice versa. The same was possible with all the "opposite" dualities or individuations—man and woman, up and down, left and right. And each of these dualities had their own smaller dualities. For example, a woman or man had the dualities of sad or happy, and so on. And even happy had its range of very happy and not so happy, and so on. And the total of these experiences is the experience of the One. But for our discussion now, we will look at the Initial Duality that first came of the One.

Now let us get back to the question of what energy is. From One, we have the Initial Duality. Now let us call that duality spirit and anti-spirit. By the way, quantum scientists have discovered that subatomic particles all have opposites—a proton has an anti-proton, for instance. But in our part of the universe, the anti-particles are not present because anti-particles destroy particles when they meet. Scientists talk of these as the matter and anti-matter of the universe.

Now the part of One that is spirit individuates itself again into infinite little parts or spirits. Quantum physicists have also seen that, although they call a subatomic particle a particle, it is not really a "thing," but rather the building block of other things. And although a subatomic particle has a wave-like behavior and a particle-like behavior, there are no particles actually running around and no waves actually fluctuating. You cannot visualize a subatomic "particle." You can only calculate it and experience it. Subatomic particles behave as spirit would. Why do they do that? Now do you see what pure energy is? It is spirit. Everything in this part of the universe is energy. Energy is matter—one and the same thing ($E=mc^2$). Spirit is energy. And hence, spirit is matter. You see, there are no clear lines of definition and separation. All That Is really is One. Individuation is not separation. Think of individuation as possessing many dimensions, not as separation into many separate things. And think of the world as dimensions or facets of the same One, not as separate things.

The other part of the universe, for everything is a duality, is the anti-universe, made up of anti-matter. But that is another topic altogether. The point is that you now can trace the origins and explanation of the universe and its link to spirit and to All. You now remember who you really are, who we really are, and why you, we, did all this. You now also know that what the Source is, You Are. It is a very complex topic, and you do not need to understand it fully. Just knowing the truth is enough; you do not need to explain it in detail.

—I am wealth. I am abundance. I am joy.—

All other things held constant, to the extent that an individual or society is One, so will it have wealth and happiness.

Again, the greatest advice that can be given to you now is this: meditate daily. Soon—maybe on your first meditation, maybe later— you will come to experience this Oneness, and you will be amazed at it! It cannot be spoken of, only experienced. This is a journey only you can take on your own. Meditation takes you in to meet your Self and infinity. It cannot be explained, only experienced.

Now, if you are one with the Source and All That Is, guess what else you are? You are abundant by nature! Let's have a look at your abundance.

CHAPTER 20
Abundance: You Have It All

YOU HAVE SEEN THAT YOU ARE ONE with the Source, one with All That Is. This makes you abundant. You have also seen how you created reality out of the quantum field simply by using your thoughts, states of being, words, and actions. You have also seen how anything is possible when you believe and choose consistently and with clarity. All this makes you abundant. At your highest level, you are naturally ever-presently abundant—there is nothing you have to do, and you cannot be anything other than abundant.

Let us look at aspects of this abundance and how to make it materialize in your life. You are One with All That Is.

Spend your money gladly, cheerfully, and with excitement. Whether you are buying items or paying bills, be glad that you are doing it. Money runs away from those who feel it is in shortage, those who have negativity toward its use.

—I am wealth. I am abundance. I am joy.—

Nature is capable of giving you all your desires without losing anything itself. Scarcity is not real; it only appears where we choose to see it.

—I am wealth. I am abundance. I am joy.—

The Source of all that is can never run out of creative power and ability. A million times what has been created can be created again. The supply is unlimited.

—I am wealth. I am abundance. I am joy.—

Thoughts of scarcity take away abundance from your life. They manifest scarcity into the physical world. To avoid scarcity, eliminate all thoughts of competition and instead choose creation. Competition is a statement to the universe that you believe your survival is at risk, and that there is not enough. So are thoughts of cheating, squeezing, manipulating, and taking advantage of people, paying unfairly, coveting other people's property, envy, and the like. These thoughts only create non-wealth consciousness and cause scarcity. You can get temporarily rich this way, but you cannot rise to your full potential this way, and indeed, you may even fall.

—I am wealth. I am abundance. I am joy.—

Never look at the visible supply. Look always at the limitless riches in formless substance, and know that they are coming to you as fast as you can receive and use them. Nobody, by cornering the visible supply, can prevent you from getting what is yours.

—*Wallace D. Wattles*

—I am wealth. I am abundance. I am joy.—

A Happy Pocket Full of Money

You are made in the image and likeness of the Source, God. Abundance and affluence are your natural states. In the deepest part of you, you already know this to be so. All you need do is to remember this in order to experience what you truly are.

—I am wealth. I am abundance. I am joy.—

The universe has more than enough business and wealth for everyone—way more than enough. People are not poor because nature is poor. People are poor because their wealth consciousness is poor. Even in a billion lifetimes, let alone one lifetime, you cannot possibly exhaust the wealth given to you freely by life. But you can "fail" to receive it by your own thoughts, words, actions, and, most of all, your chosen states of being—your "I Am" statements and the truths that you uphold about yourself. The idea that a person fails in wealth-building because of competition or other such circumstances is illusionary. The so-called competition and negative circumstances are created by those who believe in scarcity. They come to these people in the most amazing ways to fulfill their self-set limits.

—I am wealth. I am abundance. I am joy.—

Abundance, affluence, and wealth are your birthright.

—I am wealth. I am abundance. I am joy.—

Poverty is a transgression of the laws of the universe. The universe, by law and design, is not a place where poverty is natural—it is an abnormality.

—I am wealth. I am abundance. I am joy.—

Do not scare money away by saying and thinking there is not enough of it.

—I am wealth. I am abundance. I am joy.—

You cannot even begin to ponder the infinite vastness of the readily and freely available supply of value-creation material and energy you have access to.

—I am wealth. I am abundance. I am joy.—

Do not manipulate people and things. That is competitive thinking. Creative thinking is more effective and true to the nature of abundance. Competitive thinking makes you think in terms of scarcity that has to be fought against, and that is what you get. Why would you wish to create scarcity?

—I am wealth. I am abundance. I am joy.—

Economics teaches about scarcity of resources. None of that is true! Economics was "invented" at a time when people believed in scarcity. This belief caused a world of scarcity and perpetuated an illusion of scarcity, thus fulfilling the prophecy of economists. Economics is derived from observation. It totally ignores First Cause, spirit, and state of being. We are only now beginning to see that certain resources can never run out. For example, software, music, or other digital content downloaded or broadcast cannot run out. How do you run out of a software download? No matter how many copies you download, there still remains that original copy that everyone is downloading. One copy multiplies as much as is needed without costing the maker any more money. We will soon come to know experientially that, if enough of us put our minds to it, we can re-grow the entire earth's forests in a few years, create "new" water, or do anything else. Do not believe in the economics of scarcity. If you do, it will become true for you—a self-fulfilling prophecy of scarcity.

Economics developed at the time when scarcity was all there was. That is why it is failing to apply this new quantum economics to businesses and calculations today. If you do not believe this, have a look at history. At one time, people were sure the earth was flat, and all their "evidence" at the time told them this was true. Then they believed the sun rotated around the earth, and all their "evidence" at the time told them this was true. Yet we now know that the earth rotates around the sun. Or do we? In other words, whatever we hold as true is what becomes true, even though it may not be the Ultimate Truth. When we start questioning, we uncover a more "correct" truth that is closer to Ultimate Truth. There is always room for more revelation; you cannot say that your current answer is the Ultimate Truth. Our finite minds are incapable of taking in the totality of Ultimate Truth, which is infinite. We can only take small segments of it at a time.

Never stop learning. Always be humble with what you know now, and you will come to know more. Scientists are only now discovering that this universe is not four-dimensional, but multi-dimensional, like a hologram. It is our senses that are four-dimensional (length, width, height, and time). Your Self is multi-dimensional, but your senses on the physical plane are, as for most people, four-dimensional in their capabilities. The universe itself is multi-dimensional and that is how all possibilities exist all together. Think about that carefully. Scarcity is not a reality; it is a perception of an aspect of that holographic universe. You can always choose which aspect you wish to perceive and experience by choosing what you wish to believe and hold as unquestioningly true.

—I am wealth. I am abundance. I am joy.—

There is an infinite source of supply. When you don't have what you would like, know that your thoughts are at fault, not the universe. Accept full responsibility honestly and make amends. But never talk or think of lack or shortages, for in that thought is the cause of lack and shortages.

—I am wealth. I am abundance. I am joy.—

Being broke is temporary. But being poor is a mental condition, a disease of the mind, and it is more lasting. Yet all can be overcome.

—I am wealth. I am abundance. I am joy.—

How much is enough? Considering the fact that supply is infinite, enough is probably the amount that allows you to live as you would wish to live, whether you are working or not. You then choose when to play and when to work as you like, not because you need money. Hence, conditionality and need move away from you and let you explore other aspects of life other than money.

—I am wealth. I am abundance. I am joy.—

Abundance is all there is, and sharing, not owning, is the way to receive this abundance.

—I am wealth. I am abundance. I am joy.—

Competition is unnecessary. It is a statement of scarcity, a fallacy.

—I am wealth. I am abundance. I am joy.—

Competition in a business is a statement of scarcity and a bringer of scarcity. Creativity is a statement of abundance, the natural state. Shift from competitive to creative thought and see how that works for you.

—I am wealth. I am abundance. I am joy.—

This is a universe of abundance. No one is going to "take your share" or "beat you to it." There is more than enough for everyone. The only time there is not enough, the only time when you are "beaten to it," is when you think and act competitively instead of thinking and acting creatively and trusting in the abundant nature of the Source.

Thinking and acting competitively makes it harder for you to follow the laws of the universe correctly—especially the laws of cause and effect, the process of life expressing images of the mind, and the power of certainty and faith. Thinking creatively and non-competitively helps you be in agreement with these universal laws and processes.

—I am wealth. I am abundance. I am joy.—

To you the earth yields her fruit, and you shall not want if you but know how to fill your hands. It is in exchanging these gifts of the earth that you shall find abundance and be satisfied. Yet unless the exchange be in love and kindly justice it will lead some to greed and others to hunger.

—Kahlil Gibran

—I am wealth. I am abundance. I am joy.—

Out of abundance He took abundance and still abundance remains.

—Upanishads

—I am wealth. I am abundance. I am joy.—

All other things held constant, to the extent that an individual or society sees, believes in, and acts in abundance, so will it have wealth and happiness.

Again, meditate. It is the fastest way for you to know experientially how abundant you are. These higher concepts cannot be explained and fully understood intellectually. They can only be experienced. They can be talked about using symbols like words, but the full appreciation and knowing can only come from experience. And

Abundance: You Have It All

all you need to do is go within, meditate, and all the experience you need will be right there. One day—maybe with your first meditation, maybe later—it will definitely happen. This is what the Buddha called enlightenment—the realization of the One.

There is no point to life if you have no joy, for life is joy and joy is life. But what is happiness, and how does it become you?

CHAPTER 21

Happiness: Life Is Joy— Joy Is Life

T HE ESSENTIAL NATURE OF LIFE IS JOY. Joy is what life is made up of and vice versa. It is the natural state of all beings. Anything with life (and everything has life) has joy as its natural state. It is how we are born as children, with a natural ability to live life with carefree abandon and joy. You can recapture that nature and extend it.

The same laws of the universe that apply to wealth also apply to happiness. You have already seen many of these laws in previous chapters. Apply them to happiness just as you applied them to wealth. This is especially so with the law of cause and effect. If you wish to be happy, cause another to be happy. Conditionality is also an illusion when it comes to happiness. You are not happy because of certain conditions; certain conditions come into being because you are happy. Happy thoughts and images also result in happy external events and conditions. Remember, too, to act as if you are happy, and to be grateful for all, even before you experience it. And remember to practice detachment. Perhaps the most important thing to remember is that the external world fashions itself to match your internal world. If you are not happy with the external world, seek what you are not happy with internally; then choose to be happy about it. Love yourself and the world will love you. Be happy with yourself, and the world will be happy about and with you.

How do you do these things? You just do them, Now. Do not complicate this; it is simple. Make the decision right now to be happy with yourself and to love yourself.

Happiness is a decision. Decide now to be in the state of happiness, and all else will follow.

—I am wealth. I am abundance. I am joy.—

Happiness is a continuum of moments that are not resisted. If you resist a moment, you will not be happy with it. Also, what you resist persists; what you accept and bring into your light reveals itself and lets go of you. Unconditional love, acceptance, detachment, and tolerance—all these lead to happiness.

—I am wealth. I am abundance. I am joy.—

Sadness and joy are different grades of the same thing. They just appear to be different things. Hot and cold are actually just gradations of the same thing called temperature. When you express yourself and your desires, you have joy. When you do not, you have sadness.

—I am wealth. I am abundance. I am joy.—

Follow your desires.

—I am wealth. I am abundance. I am joy.—

It has been said that happiness comes from you making things happen for you instead of you waiting for things to happen to and for you.

—I am wealth. I am abundance. I am joy.—

Balance your body, mind, and soul. Without a balance, you may become unhappy. Spend time doing things related to all these three aspects of you. For your body, take care of it, have fun with it, enjoy it, use it, exercise it, feed it well, rest it. For your mind, continuously feed it with new knowledge, exercise it, think properly and deliberately, rest it. For your spirit, learn about it, exercise it, meditate and get in contact with it. And for all three, listen to them and honor what they tell you, and love them.

—I am wealth. I am abundance. I am joy.—

Joy is your true nature. Another word for your soul is joy.
Soul = Joy = Freedom = Soul. The lack of joy is the lack of expression of the soul.

—I am wealth. I am abundance. I am joy.—

Protect and nurture the environment, nature. Whether in your immediate surroundings or around the world, do your part and do more. The health of your environment influences the health of your Self, which influences the joy of your Self. The beauty and comfort of your environment also influence your joy. The joy and harmony in all things that make up your environment influence your joy and harmony. It is all connected.

—I am wealth. I am abundance. I am joy.—

Love, laughter, sharing, enthusiasm, optimism, and lightheartedness—these things make a person happy. Choose to be these things, and you will be happy. Just make the choice to be these things from now on.

—I am wealth. I am abundance. I am joy.—

Find the humor in everything. Everything has humor in it, even the most "serious" things. Try it. At first, it may be hard to find humor, but soon it will become second nature after you get used to it. And it will liberate you.

—I am wealth. I am abundance. I am joy.—

Happiness is not found in a circumstance or event. Each event is just that—an event. You choose to experience an event as a happy one or an unhappy one.

—I am wealth. I am abundance. I am joy.—

When faced with an event, choose the response that will bring happiness.

—I am wealth. I am abundance. I am joy.—

Happiness comes from creating instead of reacting.

—I am wealth. I am abundance. I am joy.—

Happiness comes from truthful observation of what is within you and outside of you. It comes from being truthful to yourself and everything else outside of you. The truth, literally, sets you free.

—I am wealth. I am abundance. I am joy.—

Choose to be happy. You are not your circumstances—that is a powerful illusion. Your circumstances are you—that is a truth. Try to understand this. When you change you, you change your circumstances.

—I am wealth. I am abundance. I am joy.—

Choose to like yourself, to love yourself. Scream aloud several times: "I love myself!"—and do it convincingly! Just make the choice, now. Do not complicate it. It is a simple choice. What if there is something about yourself that you do not like? Start liking it, and then change it. See, what you resist will never let go of you. If a person tells you not to think of the color red, you will find yourself thinking of the color red. Whatever it is that you do not like about yourself, stop resisting it. Instead, accept it, bring it into your light, love it, and look at it calmly with detachment. Smile with it and befriend it. It will then reveal its secrets to you and let go of you. But you must continuously choose to like yourself fully at all times.

This means that you start thinking about the thoughts you have about yourself. Whenever you get a thought about yourself that is negative, end it instantly and go positive. Be deliberate in thought. You become what you think about most often. If you think unloving thoughts about yourself, you become an unloved person. Both you and other people will be unable to love you. It is very simple. Choose well, for it is all within your power to the extent that you choose clearly, consistently, and with faith. If you consistently think you are ugly, unwanted, unable to do this or that, it will be so. The universe will conspire to make the powerful thoughts that you have of yourself become true. The conditions to make them true will arise. Change your mind, and change your world. Choose well.

—I am wealth. I am abundance. I am joy.—

Live Now, Here. As Harry Potter was advised by his headmaster, Albus Dumbledore, in *Harry Potter and the Philosopher's Stone*, "It does not do to dwell on dreams and forget to live." Harry found a magic mirror that showed, according to Dumbledore, the "deepest and most desperate desires of our hearts... but not knowledge or truth." Dumbledore then cautioned Harry against its use, for although it may have felt comfortable to spend all day dreaming of desires, doing so is not living. Living is what allows life to express itself, and with expression comes joy. It is okay to dream, but live life Now, Here, because the only place you can live life is Now, Here. Dumbledore then explained that the happiest person is the one who looks into the magic mirror and sees only him or herself, exactly as they are Now, Here. Think about that.

—I am wealth. I am abundance. I am joy.—

There is an old saying that says, "When you laugh, the world laughs with you, but when you cry, you cry alone." Stop crying and start laughing.

—I am wealth. I am abundance. I am joy.—

Keep it simple.

—I am wealth. I am abundance. I am joy.—

Have enthusiasm, live with passion. How? Choose to do so. Just do it.

—I am wealth. I am abundance. I am joy.—

Change your mind. Start seeing how good things really are and you will have joy. Look at the light and you will never see the darkness. Change your mind; change what you think you see. You can look at the same thing and see a happy picture instead of an unhappy one. See the good in everything. See the magic. That is what happy people do.

—I am wealth. I am abundance. I am joy.—

Joy is what happens to us when we allow ourselves to recognize how good things really are.

—*Marianne Williamson*

—I am wealth. I am abundance. I am joy.—

Cultivate your relationships with people. Happy people, statistically and quite obviously, have healthy and happy relationships with friends and family. Love is a powerful force. Be friendly and show unconditional love and you will make friends and have many fantastic relationships. That said, you must always remember that you need nothing outside of yourself to be happy. Do not become a person that relies on others to be happy—that is an addiction and a falsehood, not to mention an unfair pressure placed on others that will only lead to eventual unhappiness.

Love yourself and recognize that your love for others must be unconditional and free. Then be friendly. And keep your freedom of choice—any relationship where you lose your freedom of choice is an unhealthy one that leads to unhappiness. Stable, fair, free, and loving relationships on all levels lead to happiness. Think about this. You do not owe anybody anything at all, ever, for any reason. Everything you do for others is a gift to them. And vice versa. Once you understand this statement deeply, you understand unconditional love, one that requires nothing in particular from others, and one that is not pressured into giving anything in particular to others. In unconditional love, all that exists are gifts given and accepted cheerfully and naturally.

—I am wealth. I am abundance. I am joy.—

From love comes joy. What is love? Love is not a bond; it is a freedom—a liberator, not a binder. It is a free expresser, not a limiter. In the presence of true love, things flourish as they are—perfect.

—I am wealth. I am abundance. I am joy.—

Fill each other's cup but drink not from one cup.

—Kahlil Gibran

—I am wealth. I am abundance. I am joy.—

Do not spend any time at all thinking about how unhappy you are or how this, that, or the other thing makes you unhappy. Remember, you become what you think of most of the time.

—I am wealth. I am abundance. I am joy.—

The less judgmental you are, the happier you become. The more forgiving you are, the happier you become.

—I am wealth. I am abundance. I am joy.—

Cherish and nurture your freedom, and let others have theirs as well. Practice unconditional love for yourself and for others. Freedom and love—these are the keys to happiness. Do not cut short your own freedom or another's. True and unconditional freedom and love are the flames that fuel creativity, trust, growth, and expression of spirit, hence joy. It is important to understand the nature of unconditional love and freedom. Love and freedom that come full of conditions go against the only constant in the universe: change. Every moment, things change. Change is growth. Conditional love resists change; it is the love of an idea, not a person. It is the love of a past known moment and not a future unknown moment. It is full of fear that the conditions will one day not be met. That fear attracts the very thing that is feared. This is evident all around our world today.

Finally, yet importantly, conditional love and conditioned freedom take away the power to choose happiness no matter what the event is. Happiness is a choice. People who understand this are able to face any situation with joy. Conditionality makes it harder for you to do this. To be happy, start to understand and practice unconditional love and freedom. Start to enjoy watching others grow as they choose to grow, not as you choose them to grow. Start to enjoy the unknown moment of the future and stop clinging to a past known moment. Start creating instead of reacting.

—I am wealth. I am abundance. I am joy.—

It is not how much you do but how much love you put into the doing and sharing with others that is important. Try not to judge people. If you judge others then you are not giving love.

—Mother Teresa

—I am wealth. I am abundance. I am joy.—

Give, give, and give. Giving is another powerful key to happiness.

—I am wealth. I am abundance. I am joy.—

Give unconditionally whatever a person needs in the moment. The point is to do something, however small, and show you care through your actions by giving your time.

—Mother Teresa

—I am wealth. I am abundance. I am joy.—

You give but little when you give of your possessions. It is when you give of yourself that you truly give.

—Kahlil Gibran

—I am wealth. I am abundance. I am joy.—

One of the best ways to become wealthy and happy is by practicing meditation every day. Meditation puts you in touch with your higher Self, and the teachings in this book become you, experientially, in every cell of your body. They are no longer theoretical constructs, for they become you. You no longer have to struggle to practice and remember them, for they are you. Start meditating, and one day soon, you will have this happen to you. The recommended meditation technique here is Vipassana (mindfulness/insight) meditation.

—I am wealth. I am abundance. I am joy.—

Spread your joy. Make others happy. It will come back to you seven-fold.

—I am wealth. I am abundance. I am joy.—

Whatever you wish others to recognize and see in you, recognize it and see it in them.

—I am wealth. I am abundance. I am joy.—

Compliment others every day. Find something to compliment. Do it genuinely.

—I am wealth. I am abundance. I am joy.—

Consider this. In Ultimate Reality, there is no right or wrong, no should or should not. There are no accidents or coincidences or good or bad luck—all events are perfect outcomes of universal law that never fails or errs. It is our choices and goals that make a thing right or wrong, good or bad, in the pursuit of that goal or choice. For example, killing is a perfect outcome of universal law and it is not, in itself, wrong. But if, as a society, we wish to promote peace, happiness, and prosperity, then killing is wrong. Our choices make a thing right or wrong. But on its own and without our choices, a thing is just a perfect outcome of universal law.

Also consider this. Change is all there is. That includes what society considers acceptable or not. Even what looks like an acceptable form of behavior now was at some time in the past unacceptable and will someday become unacceptable again. And vice versa. Also, what is acceptable here may not be acceptable somewhere else or at another time or place. Think about this on a global, racial, sexual, economic status, and age scale. Then ask yourself why.

Also consider this. To the extent that you make your own choices instead of taking the choices passed on to you by others, you will be happy, growing, and free.

What is "should"? What is "can"? Why? Who are you? Why? Why? Think about all these things. Think about them with detachment. Observe them truly. Within those answers, you will find liberation, power, love, and happiness. The more you choose for yourself what your life events are, based on your truths and not the truths of others, the happier you are.

—I am wealth. I am abundance. I am joy.—

You learn to love by loving. You just do it. It is not complicated unless you complicate it. So do not complicate it.

—I am wealth. I am abundance. I am joy.—

You need not wait a single moment to start being happy. How fantastic is that! Right now, right here, you can make that choice. You need nothing outside of yourself to be happy and wealthy—it is all inside. The outside simply responds to allow you to experience your internal state physically.

—I am wealth. I am abundance. I am joy.—

The truth is, the happy get happier because they know how to be happy, and the troubled get more troubled because they pour all their life energy into their troubles.

—*Susan Page*

—I am wealth. I am abundance. I am joy.—

Remember the dangers of wanting. Never want happiness or anything else. A state of want is a perpetual state of never having and a declaration of not having. Instead of wanting, desire and intend with detachment.

—I am wealth. I am abundance. I am joy.—

The more love you give away, the more of it you get in return.

—I am wealth. I am abundance. I am joy.—

Your joy is your sorrow unmasked… When you are joyous, look deep into your heart and you shall find that it is only that which has given you sorrow that is giving you joy. When you are sorrowful, look again in your heart, and you shall see that in truth you are weeping for that which has been your delight.

—*Kahlil Gibran*

—I am wealth. I am abundance. I am joy.—

Do not complain. Either to yourself or to others. What good does it do, except to highlight negativity and cause it?

—I am wealth. I am abundance. I am joy.—

Smile. Just smile. Try it; it makes you happy. Smile because you know how life works—because you know the Big Secret.

—I am wealth. I am abundance. I am joy.—

Real joy comes from within, from Being. Pleasure and pain come from without, from things outside of you. Joy never stops being joy. It is the nature of spirit, of being. It is not affected by external things. Once you are present in Now and aware and in touch with your Self, the joy will be everywhere in you and it shall never stop. It never has stopped and never can stop anyway, but you can be blind to it by not being Here, Now, fully present. Joy is an eternal state, in Now. It is not in the past or future, for those are "times" that do not exist, except in the mind.

Pleasure and pain, on the other hand are external. They are also complimentary. The same thing that gives you pleasure gives you pain. Think about it. When whatever external thing gives you pleasure is not there, you feel pain—the pain of not having it. The same thing gives you pleasure and pain. When the thing that gives you pain is not there, you feel pleasure. The same thing gives you both. All external things do this, and that is why people often feel unsatisfied. However, once you touch your Self and live Now, real joy comes to the surface, and that can never change to pain. From that point on, everything will become enjoyable; even the most "painful" things will cease to bring suffering to you, and you will marvel at all life. Joy is Being, and Being is Is-ness, Now. From that point on, you shall be happy with all being, resisting no present moment, but creating your next moments in a powerful way through true choice.

Resisting Is-ness is futile. Resisting Now is painful. What do you expect to gain by resisting what Is? You cannot undo it. So why bother? Yet when you touch your Self and feel joy, you shall not need any intellectual conviction to stop resisting Now. You shall just naturally love all being.

Why does the same thing give you both pain and pleasure? It is because your mind lives outside the moment of Now. For example, if you like a certain thing that gives you pleasure, when you have that thing, you enjoy it (unless you worry about losing it). When you do not have it and you let your mind escape Now and go into the past and future, thinking, you start getting into "problems." You get lost in thoughts like: "It was great when I had that thing, and I really wish I had it now. I look forward to when I will next have it. I do not like not having it now." When you think like that, you totally miss the joy of Now, what Is. And that "gap" between Now, Is-ness, and a past and future that only exist in your mind is the cause of pain, anxiety, and dissatisfaction.

Joy is always in the moment of Now. It is ever-present, but you can choose not to see it. When you are out of mind, of no mind, you are Being, Now, in harmony with all else that Is, Now. In that state, you are in the best position to enjoy Now and also to create the next Now in the most powerful way, free of worry, anxiety, and negativity. Your mind is a tool, and you should activate it to create an intention of the next Now. This very quick and detached thinking should not take any more than a few seconds every now and then. If you use your mind to constantly ramble on inside your head thinking about the past and future, all you do is live in the past, worry about the future, and lose the joy of Now. And anyway, that is not a good formula for creating a future. All problems exist only in the mind; they cannot exist in Now. In Now, you always pass. You cannot fail Now. Not two seconds from now, or five hours from now, but right Now. All problems exist outside of Now, in your mind; they arise when you use your mind incorrectly.

—I am wealth. I am abundance. I am joy.—

All other things held constant, to the extent that an individual or society loves unconditionally, causes each other happiness, and lives Now, so will it have wealth and happiness.

Remember, life is a celebration, and joy makes for celebration. Joy is spirit being expressed in the ways it likes and desires. Express your spirit, and let others express theirs!

Well, we started with money, went on to larger things, and now we shall go back to money. Money is not the real thing; it is only a symbol of the real wealth inside us. We have so far been looking at what makes up the real thing. Even though money is not the real thing, we still need to know how to use it. It is a full circle, a full cycle. Money is the end of many other things that make up wealth consciousness; but it is the beginning of the experiencing of wealth consciousness as material wealth.

Money is a symbol of wealth and the beginning of the experiencing of wealth, so that we may know what wealth tastes like experientially. Money has two uses: it allows us to exchange our gifts and it allows us to experience wealth. Through this experience, we are able to increase our wealth consciousness and love it even more. Wealth consciousness begets wealth and money, which begets wealth consciousness, and the cycle goes on. It is a full circle, a full cycle. So, we go back to money.

CHAPTER 22

Money: How to Use the Symbol

THIS IS WORTH REPEATING, for repetition causes internalization. Money is not the real thing; it is only a symbol of the real
wealth inside us. We have so far been looking at what makes up
the real thing. Even though money is not the real thing, we still need
to know how to use it. It is a full circle, a full cycle. Money is the end
of many other things that make up wealth consciousness; but it is the
beginning of the experiencing of wealth consciousness as material
wealth.

Money is a symbol of wealth and the beginning of the experiencing of wealth, so that we may know what wealth tastes like experientially. Money has two primary uses: it allows us to exchange our
gifts and it allows us to experience wealth. Through this experience,
we are able to increase our wealth consciousness and love it even more.
Wealth consciousness begets wealth and money, which begets wealth
consciousness, and the cycle goes on. It is a full circle, a full cycle.

Let us spend some time on money.

Do not be ashamed of money. Do not act as if you are ashamed
of it. Hiding money, handling it as if it were dirty, being dishonest

with money, and other similar attitudes and acts are all detrimental to you if you wish to acquire wealth. This is not a call for you to start bragging; it is a call for you to be honest in all ways with your money. Be honest to the money and about the money. Things that lead to dishonesty with and about money, or things that stem from it, eventually damage your wealth.

—I am wealth. I am abundance. I am joy.—

I love money and money loves me! Scream this enthusiastically, repeatedly, every now and then, until all feelings of ridicule and guilt and fear of money eventually leave you.

—I am wealth. I am abundance. I am joy.—

As you become wealthier materially, it may be in your best interests, depending on where you live, to have off-shore specialists look into your affairs and structure them for maximum safety and benefits. Vehicles like trusts and holding companies in off-shore jurisdictions have enabled wealthy people to have peace and continued prosperity for generations. Remember that, presently, we do need governments, and we must pay our fair part to keep them running. It is to our advantage to have government. But government was created to serve people fairly, and when it ceases to act in such a way, then it becomes your biggest hindrance and stressor. And because governments are run by human beings capable of error, they can sometimes oppress instead of enhance. They can sometimes waste instead of create. They can sometimes make laws that are unfair and unjust, even if only for a portion of the population. That is why it is to your advantage to structure your affairs very early in such a way that you are both within and outside of government control, instead of remaining totally within it.

That freedom is sometimes the key to growing wealth. Sometimes it can even save you from losing your wealth. This call to look off-shore is not a call to greed and anarchy; it is a call for freedom and fairness. If you cannot guarantee that your government will be fair to you at all times, you should guarantee that you can step aside or outside safely in the event that it is not. There is no point in taking an unnecessary and lethal blow to your finances in the name of patriotism. Options enable choice. Without options, you cannot choose. Always ensure that you have options in everything.

In regard to wealth and many other matters, the options you should seek to guarantee are the option to travel at will when you need to, the option to live in a place where you are happy and safe, and the option to handle your finances in the way that best suits you and your society, in your fair judgment. The way to guarantee these freedoms, these options, is to have two legal passports from two separate countries, legal residency capability in two countries with unrelated jurisdiction, off-shore bank accounts, and off-shore holding or processing companies.

Asset and income protection arrangements are much like insurance, by the way. You do not insure your house against fire after it burns down; you do it before the fire, in case a fire ever comes your way. But never forget that you have an interest in paying something fair in taxes to keep your government healthy. Even if you find yourself in a position whereby you can escape all taxes, it is a good idea to pay about 10 percent of your income in taxes voluntarily.

—I am wealth. I am abundance. I am joy.—

Pay your fair share of tax cheerfully, for it keeps the society alive and in functioning order. It is up to you to determine what is fair. Over the ages, sages and teachers have taught that 10 percent is a fair amount. Even religious texts have recommended similar tithing arrangements. Mathematically, 10 percent is also optimal for all involved.

—I am wealth. I am abundance. I am joy.—

Of your income, devise ways to ensure that you pay about 10 percent of it in taxes, that you give about 10 percent to charity, that you invest 10 percent in long-term growth and wealth-building investments. Then use the remaining 70 percent to live, grow, and enjoy life. The added bonus to you using your money to enjoy life is that as you spend money on things, you make others wealthier!

As you get immensely richer, if you can live on a lower percentage of your income, then give and invest more. These ratios were designed, over the ages, to give you and your world the best growth and wealth possibilities for all.

—I am wealth. I am abundance. I am joy.—

Keep accurate personal and business accounts. Know what happens to your money and where it goes and comes from. Knowing is the first step to mastery of anything, and not knowing where your money goes is crippling. If your cash out exceeds your cash in, your upkeep—staying alive—will be your downfall. You cannot plan and analyze what you do not know.

Be careful, however, about managing your finances. This is not a call to stringent penny-pinching and miserliness. Do not let your keeping of accurate financial records turn you into a miser, a person who believes that money is in short supply. Keeping accounts is just that—keeping accounts.

—I am wealth. I am abundance. I am joy.—

Surround yourself with very wise advisors, associates, and employees. The wise person keeps wiser counsel. Have wise counsel in all fields—business, accounting, tax, law, trusts, investments, etc. Pay them well, pay them on performance, and give them bonuses when they deserve it. Remember, wealth usually flows to those with right knowledge, but the person who gets that wealth does not necessarily have to be the possessor of the knowledge. The wealthy person is often the one who brings together teams of knowledgeable people, even though he or she may not possess the knowledge personally.

—I am wealth. I am abundance. I am joy.—

Learn to multiply your efforts. One of the best ways to do that is to delegate massively. Delegate almost everything. Every person has certain unique capabilities. But they also share many other things with everybody else. For example, Einstein's special gift was in physics. That is where he varied most from the rest of us. But on all other things, that variance was very low. He walked, wrote, saw, cleaned the house, and did other chores just a little better or a little worse than we all do. Now, if in a day, Einstein insisted on doing absolutely everything in his "business," from thinking about physics to drawing charts that anyone else could have drawn, to sweeping his floor, he would have ended up with far less time to spend on his unique talents and therefore have realized less from them. A person's unique talents are what make the person and the world wealthy.

Wealthy people usually look at themselves honestly and see what they most enjoy and what they are a whole lot better at than most other people. This is an honest look. What you are best at may be strategy, marketing, innovation, horticulture, flying, driving, or anything else. You may also be good at a whole lot of other things, maybe even slightly better than most people, but that is beside the point. The real question is: What are you fabulous at—not just good, but fabulous? The only other question is: What is it that you really enjoy and cannot stop doing? Don't say, "I can clean the floor better than my cleaner," for, even if that is true, it is self-defeating. All that matters is what you are better at, by far, than anyone else, and what you enjoy. Then do only that thing, and delegate everything else. Do not worry that people will not do the rest as well as you would have.

Imagine if Bill Gates tried to do everything at Microsoft. What good would that do him or the rest of us? A person like Bill Gates is focused on what he does best and what he enjoys most. He delegates all the rest, even if he can do some of it better than his helpers or employees can. In addition to that, people like that recognize that there are many things that other people are a lot better at doing than they themselves are. Delegation multiplies efforts and results. Put it in your thinking and your goals to delegate almost everything in your business except for the one thing you are exceptionally good at and what you most enjoy (even if it is just dreaming up new ideas).

To the extent that you delegate to the right people, so shall you become more productive and hence wealthier.

—I am wealth. I am abundance. I am joy.—

Increase the rate at which you get ideas. Read books and magazines for a few minutes each day at least. Learn to read faster—the more new ideas you get the better. Get a speed-reading course or book. To find good books, use Amazon's user ratings to see what readers like you have found useful in their lives. Read magazines in all areas of life to get a broad picture of the world. The best thing about magazines is their images; they feed your imagination and your goals.

—I am wealth. I am abundance. I am joy.—

Another way to look at the making of money is to view it as a change of thought causing a shift in the way energy in the universe is exchanged. This is not so that you may start living like this, but just so that you may see that simply changing your thought causes a rearranging of the energy in the universe that can lead to increased wealth. Let us see how that works historically.

Thousands of years ago, people were hunters and gatherers. This was a dangerous and unpredictable way to live. The desire to have more stability and safety caused human beings to think: Why do I have to chase after these goats in the wild every day? That led to the idea that goats could be kept at home, domesticated. Now, instead of chasing after goats every day across the grass plains, man brought them together in an enclosure and fed them the same grass from the plains. Even before this new idea, there was always an abundance of grass, land, and goats; but no one had thought of changing their arrangement, of domesticating the goats. The idea simply changed the way the different forms of energy were exchanged. A desire for a better life caused a thought that caused betterment in the standard of living, using the same material that had always been there. A change of thought pattern caused this.

Next, human beings desired to reduce their hardships further by acquiring items they needed but did not have. They first did this by going to war with tribes that had these items. Then they desired a much safer way to acquire these items, which led to the idea that they could trade. Again, they improved their lives simply by rearranging their thoughts, causing a change in the way energy in various forms was exchanged.

Trade went along fine. The only problem was the long distances people had to carry their goats to exchange them for a bag of wheat in the next village. The desire to exchange faster and more efficiently led to the idea that, instead of everyone walking all over the place, people could instead meet at one central spot and show all their goods and trade. Thus a market was formed. Again, look at it closely. All the ingredients had always existed, but the idea that it could be done had not. The desire for something better caused the idea that caused a shift in the way energy forms were exchanged. Remember the law that says energy is neither created nor destroyed, it only changes form.

A market did not drop from the heavens on these people. They simply changed their thought patterns, and it was done.

Today, the desire to trade even faster has caused us to have currency markets and stock exchanges. Imagine the time when a trader had to walk for half a day to the market, sell one cow, then walk back home. Next came trucks, and farmers could drive several cows to the market and be back home early enough to do another trip. Then came futures and options exchanges, which enabled people to buy and sell thousands of livestock futures and options in seconds without having to get up or move a single cow! Yet nothing dropped from the heavens. It was all right there. People just desired differently, and that desire took an infinite coordination of dozens of seemingly unrelated events to end up with a high-tech futures and options market with no need to move the cow at the time of trade.

The sequencing of everything needed to end up with a result that enabled faster trade and better profitability was unpredictable. But because the desire was there, nature fulfilled it. But let us go back to the past. The agrarian revolution came along and people, from their desire for more wealth, ended up with ways to improve farming. Again, they simply desired, and that desire led to thought, and what had always been there was rearranged. Nothing dropped from the heavens. But even then, it took a king three generations to build a good-sized home and accumulate a fair collection of possessions. The average person did not even think it was possible for them to live in a multi-room brick house with certain amenities—that was for kings and queens.

Today, life is different. We are born assuming, from observation, that a house is something that we shall automatically have to live in, and that we shall automatically have clothes and certain other things that were reserved for royalty in the past. It does not even cross your mind for a moment that you will lack certain things, yet people in the past struggled for generations to get those same things. We have a certainty that they did not have.

The point here is to see the powerful effects of certainty on an individual level and on a wider scale. Certainty of thought causes massive shifts in the way energy is rearranged. A massive up-shift in certainty of thought and in desire for something better always leads to a massive shift in the way energy is rearranged for a better life.

Take, for example, the emergence of the IT boom. You had Bill Gates and hundreds of other young people making massive amounts of wealth in very short periods. People became billionaires in few years, instead of the four generations it used to take. And as young people fresh out of college watched this happen, they believed they could do it too. And many of them believed. And a whole range of new businesses were formed in no time at all. Young people in their twenties were becoming millionaires by the dozens every day. Yet nothing new dropped from the heavens in those few years. All it took was massive desire, belief, and change of thought. Then the energy that was always there in various forms was rearranged into a whole bunch of new forms that led to wealth.

And just as millions of people today live better than a few kings lived in the past, the very near future will have billions of average people living better than millionaires live today. And nothing new will be dropped from the heavens. We will simply desire better, have certainty on a higher level because we are now beginning to understand how it all works. We will change our thoughts the right way, and it will just happen in unpredictable and powerful ways.

All that needs to exist is right here, and we have it all. The energy packets that make up everything around us, including our bodies, have an unlimited capability to take unlimited and unimaginable forms as long as the desire is there. They have their own intelligence, and they obey our desires with a skill that we cannot imagine. If you analyze any substance at all, from light to thought to metal to flesh, it is all made up of energy packets that "collect" into atoms, cells, and so on. But the amazing thing about these energy packets is that, unlike the forms that they build up, they are not confined in time and space. In other words, they can move from point A to B without crossing the space in between. And they are not confined within the object that they make up.

In other words, the energy packets making up your finger right now are not the same ones that will make it up in a few seconds. They can flash up in your finger then flash up in another person's belly a moment later or in a light bulb in your house. You do not have your own bunch of energy packets, so to speak. In fact, they are not really particles in the sense that you think of particles. You are forever sharing these packets with everyone and everything else at all times. And they can "travel" forward and backward in time. This is what we, and all matter, are made up of—energy packets flashing in specific patterns to form the appearance of shapes. The information that dictates these specific patterns is partially made up of our thoughts and, partially, the thoughts of the rest of the universe.

That is why medicine is now discovering that our thoughts are very much linked to our state of health. And science is discovering that nothing being observed can be observed independent of the observer, because the observer's expectations and thoughts influence the object under observation.

Money is absolutely linked to our thoughts, desires, and certainty, and to history; and science can prove that to you now. It is in your best interests to improve your own wealth consciousness and that of the world. Your becoming wealthy makes the world wealthy, and the world becoming wealthy makes you wealthy with a whole lot less effort. Look at history to prove this.

—I am wealth. I am abundance. I am joy.—

A major key to building wealth is in making your money work for you, instead of you working for your money. If you work five days a week and spend all your income without investing any of it, you will have forever lost those five days of work. Forever. Wealthy people take a portion of the income from each day and put it into investments that grow on their own, automatically and without any further work, over a long-term period. That way, a portion of each day that you work for money, that money ends up working for you for many years to come. That is a major key to wealth—getting a percentage of your income every day to work for you without your intervention.

You do this by taking at least 10 percent of your daily income before taxes and bills and putting it into a long-term investment for a minimum of about three years. Good investments include stocks, mutual funds, certain types of bank accounts that have high and above-inflation interest rates, real estate investment vehicles, bonds, royalty-producing assets, self-maintaining businesses, and so on. These investments do not require you to work for your money. You simply invest and walk away, and your money grows all on its own.

Even one dollar can turn into a million dollars in a certain number of years at a certain compound interest rate. One dollar, just one dollar, can grow into a million dollars all on its own without your intervention. You may be pleasantly surprised to know that a single dollar placed into an investment that grows at 20 percent a year will become $1 million in seventy-five years. That is just one dollar! All you need to do is leave it alone and go away—go to sleep for seventy-five years, just leave it alone. When you return it will be $1 million without any effort from you, other than your placing that single dollar at the beginning!

Now, if instead you put one dollar every single day into the same 20-percent-a-year growth investment, you will end up with $1 million in thirty-two years instead of seventy-five. In fact, a dollar a day will become $1 billion in sixty-six years. A higher interest rate will dramatically shorten that time.

This shows you that you can never have too little to start with. Whatever your income today, force yourself into the habit of investing 10 percent of it before you pay bills or taxes or anything else. Pay yourself first—it is your money and your life. And it gets even better. The 1990s was an era when stocks rose phenomenally. In that decade, over 200 stocks rose by 1,000 percent, some by up to 20,000 percent. Many fell again in 2001, but in the long-term, all good companies always rebound to even greater heights. People in the 1990s invested various amounts and found themselves wealthier for that. Some invested just $50 a week, and if that was their 10 percent, that was good enough. It grew. Others invested more. Ten thousand dollars invested just once at the beginning of 1990 in certain stocks turned out to be valued at around $5 million by the end of the decade. Others turned a few million dollars into well over a billion in the same period. All this wealth growth happened without any extra effort except putting money away into the investment.

These people were not doing anything secret; they were investing in publicly available investments. They were investing in well-selected shares in the stock market—and anyone can do this. You can do it as well, starting now. Just remember, choose your investments well, invest consistently, and put 10 percent aside from every single paycheck or other income. Consistency is the key. Compound interest will always work for you without asking anything from you. Your only part is to be consistent, to choose good investments, and to stay put for the long term. Short-term investing usually does not earn as much as long-term investing, and it is usually a lot riskier.

—I am wealth. I am abundance. I am joy.—

Taxes and the government. We need a government; that is for sure. Without governments, society would not be able, at our present stage, to organize infrastructure development, security, and so on. But there is such a thing as wasteful government or too much government. Just because it is a government does not mean it is always right, that it sets the right amount of taxes we should pay, and that it uses that money wisely without waste. So what is in our best interest, you and I, is to figure out how much we need to pay in tax. We need to keep government alive and healthy and serving us well, without paying too much to the point that we don't have enough to invest and enjoy life while government has too much and wastes it on activities like building weapons of mass destruction.

Governments across the world have tax rates ranging from zero to 80 percent. Taxes are usually a person's biggest single expenditure. Within each country, you can arrange your affairs in ways that legally minimize your tax amount with the help of professional tax advisors. Winston Churchill once said that no person has the legal or moral obligation to arrange his or her affairs so that the government can put its biggest shovel in. I personally believe that the magic formula is 10:10:10:70—that is, 10 percent of your income to taxes, 10 percent to charity, 10 percent to long-term investments, and 70 percent for your enjoyment and spending—for that is what life is all about, enjoying your life, not struggling with it.

Spending anything less than 10 percent on government will kill it, but more than that gives it too much money. It is because of this excess that we have, for example, too many deadly nuclear weapons that have never really helped us. Military expenditure is the biggest total government expenditure worldwide. Yet military expenditures do not circulate in the economy or benefit us as much as other expenditures. A nuclear missile that is built and never fired is dead money. It just stays in a silo waiting to be fired. Yet the day it is fired, it causes even more destruction. Weapons just put us in a state of fear, no matter which way you look at it. The way to prevent war is not to stop building weapons, but to eliminate borders, divisions, and economic differences. The United States would have been far weaker and less stable today if it had not united its states a couple of hundred years ago. Before becoming a federation of states, the United States had civil strife and travel and commerce barriers within itself.

Once you pay 10 percent of your money to government as taxes, don't forget to spend at least another 10 percent on charity, doing things to uplift your society and hence yourself. And invest at least 10 percent in long-term good investments. Then enjoy and spend the rest!

Be cheerful in your spending; your spending causes the increased income of others and drives the economy. Imagine what would happen if everyone stopped spending! The more we spend, the more the energy is exchanged, and the more we all get wealthy. At first, this new 10:10:10:70 arrangement may be a little difficult for some people to execute because they are spending all or almost all their money at the moment and have not arranged their affairs for optimal taxation. But within a short time, it is easy to change these habits to fit into this new format.

—I am wealth. I am abundance. I am joy.—

Knowing the real difference between an asset and a liability is another key to wealth. An asset is anything that creates net wealth or net income for you. An asset is anything that puts more money into your pocket than it took out from it. A liability is something that does not do that. A liability is anything that takes money away from your pocket without putting back into your pocket more than it took. By that definition, some of the items that people consider as assets are really liabilities. Homes that are mortgaged are liabilities (they are the bank's asset). Cars are liabilities—they take more from you in cash than they give back.

Wealthy people obviously have more assets than liabilities. That is just obvious. Can you imagine being wealthy when your true liabilities are more than your true assets?

Assets grow the wealth for wealthy people. Analyze your life and reclassify everything in it as an asset or liability as we have defined them. Always maintain more assets than liabilities; otherwise, you will have zero or negative wealth (debts). It is such a simple formula.

There is nothing wrong with buying liabilities. Indeed, many of life's most enjoyable things—beautiful homes and boats and cars—are, by our new definition, liabilities. But they make life enjoyable. So go ahead and enjoy, but never let your liabilities, as we have defined them, exceed your assets, as we have defined them; otherwise you will soon end up in negative wealth. Always maintain that positive balance. If you wish to have that nice home, the way to get it is first to work on having an asset that produces an income that is high enough to finance your mortgage. Then use it to pay for your house payments. So get assets first and use them to finance liabilities.

By the way, you do not count yourself as an asset. Getting a job to earn money to pay your mortgage is not the way. That is called working for your money, and it is an often unhealthy and dangerously entrapping cycle to get into. Your money should always work for you. The money you earn with your mind and hands, on your job or work, is to be used to acquire investments and assets. These assets and investments then generate income, on their own without much further intervention from you, to buy the liabilities for you. You do not work for your liabilities. You work for your assets, and your assets work for your liabilities.

If at present you do not know how to do that, then get books and advisors who can show you how to do that in your situation. Good assets to acquire or build include stocks, mutual funds, certain types of bank accounts that have high and above-inflation interest rates, real estate investment vehicles, bonds, royalty-producing assets, self-maintaining businesses, and so on.

—I am wealth. I am abundance. I am joy.—

Whatever you seek to know, a very good book or person exists that will give you this knowledge. For books, Amazon is a great starting point for your search. For other information, a search on Google usually gives you what you are after. In this day and age, we lack nothing. In truth, we never did; we just made up the shortages ourselves.

—I am wealth. I am abundance. I am joy.—

Live a luxurious life. Remember, life is images of the mind expressed. Keep improving your Self and your environment and surroundings with luxury and beautiful nature. It is from what is around you that many of your mental images are formed, and you therefore should have a good source of mental imagery. Luxury and a healthy environment and nature breed more wealth by breeding higher images of the mind. Live in as much luxury as you feel comfortable and happy with.

—I am wealth. I am abundance. I am joy.—

Take care of Mother Nature, the goose that lays the golden eggs. Do not pollute or destroy the environment, quickly or slowly. That is killing the same Source that enables you to be. Remember the law of cause and effect, the law that never fails. People think that they can destroy the environment, usually for self-profit, and get away with it because it is future generations that will be affected. The law of cause and effect never fails. As surely as you breathe, you reap whatever you sow, positive or negative. The only thing we do not know is how, where, and when. Sow good seeds, and you will reap a good harvest.

—I am wealth. I am abundance. I am joy.—

Money is value energy that, like all energy, lives to flow and needs flow to stay alive. Help it flow cheerfully, and it will be attracted to you.

—I am wealth. I am abundance. I am joy.—

Give the service that others need. Increase their value. We are here to serve each other, to act as growth enablers for each other. Do this in your own capacity, and money will automatically flow in.

—I am wealth. I am abundance. I am joy.—

Say to yourself and believe it: "Money loves me, and I love money." This will be true for you to the extent that you can say this comfortably and with joy, without feelings of guilt. If you find yourself guilty, find the reason why and ask yourself how true that reason is, and where it came from. To the extent that you are comfortable with money and you welcome and love it, so shall you be wealthy.

—I am wealth. I am abundance. I am joy.—

Money is an energy that allows freedom and loves freedom. It goes where there is freedom and where it is given freedom. Misers and stingy people, although they try their hardest to keep money, make it hardest for them to acquire and keep money.

—I am wealth. I am abundance. I am joy.—

Enjoy money!

—I am wealth. I am abundance. I am joy.—

Don't chase and serve money, don't be enslaved by it or seek to horde it. Instead, be with it and have a free and relaxed relationship with it. Appreciate and love it and enjoy its function and attributes, which are the enabling of freedom and the flow of value. Money, value, is energy. And like energies attract, while unlike energies repel. So have the energy attributes and vibration of money in you, and you will attract it. Do this by being happy, free, giving, and abundance-minded.

—I am wealth. I am abundance. I am joy.—

Money enjoys and loves being in the presence of wealth consciousness. It loves the company of people who love and enjoy money and, like all of life, it multiplies and flourishes in the presence of the conditions that it loves.

—I am wealth. I am abundance. I am joy.—

Treat money as a live "personality." Treat it as you would a good friend.

—I am wealth. I am abundance. I am joy.—

The more you give value—by selling valuable goods and services, by showing others how to obtain value and wealth, by buying other people's products and services, and by sharing—the more the money comes back to you through the law of cause and effect.

—I am wealth. I am abundance. I am joy.—

Dedicate a few minutes a day, every day, to the study of life, wealth, and your profession.

—I am wealth. I am abundance. I am joy.—

If one person can accomplish $1 million dollars worth of business in a given time, three people working together in harmony can accomplish much more than $3 million dollars. When in harmony, the whole is greater than the sum of its parts. Involve like-minded people in your business to multiply your efforts and income.

—I am wealth. I am abundance. I am joy.—

Be comfortable with money, feel free around it, talk about it, treat it and love it as you would a close friend. In that attitude, you will attract it. If you fear it or refuse to love it, you repel it.

—I am wealth. I am abundance. I am joy.—

Some people have a problem with loving money. But to attract money you need to love it. To attract anything, loving it is the fastest way to do it. It is also true that you also attract what you fear. When you fear money, you do not attract money; you attract whatever it is that you fear about money.

Some people say that loving money is wrong. They often say: "The love of money is the root of all evil." Analyze that statement. The love of money in itself is not evil. It can just be the root of evil. Money itself is also not evil, but it can cause coveting, greed, and subsequently crime. Loving money is perfectly healthy, as long as you do not develop that into greed and crime. In fact, loving anything, not just money, when taken in the wrong way can be the root of evil. People have killed over the love of their romantic partners, property, and religion. Yet there is nothing evil about loving partners, property, or your faith. It is never love that is wrong or the item being loved. It is only when that love is expressed in an unhealthy manner that its effects can be considered wrong.

So feel free to love money, genuinely love it, but watch yourself and do not let that love turn to greed and covetousness. But love it. Money moves to those who love it most.

Money is a lovely thing. It is a statement of abundance, not scarcity. Abundance is the natural state of the Source. It frees people to pay attention to other things in their lives. Life is fantastic, so full of so much that we have not yet explored. Money frees you to explore avenues of life that you previously did not have a chance to explore. Money also gives people the ability to express their love, to give, to create, to share, to uplift others. Love money, and it will love you.

—I am wealth. I am abundance. I am joy.—

A very important and fundamental key to wealth is multiple sources of income. Build multiple sources of income for your life. There are numerous good books on this. Multiple sources of income are your key to financial freedom. They are a manifestation of your dynamic, free, and multi-dimensional nature.

More accurately, make sure that each income stream is a business, not a job. A job is something that requires you to be there for it so that it can make money for you. A business is something that once set up, does not need you to be there to keep going or growing. A job needs you, a business does not—that is the difference. Some businesses are actually jobs. You may own a business that is a job for you. It needs you to tend to it; without your constant attention, it fails. Jobs take your time and freedom; businesses give you time and freedom. A person with multiple streams of income from multiple businesses ends up with free time that he or she can use to live well and to launch more businesses if need be. Jobs never allow such liberties—free time to diversify and to enjoy other aspects of life. So have multiple sources of income, but ensure that each source is independent of you and has been built to do well without your constant attention.

—I am wealth. I am abundance. I am joy.—

Teach wealth consciousness to your children from an early age.

—I am wealth. I am abundance. I am joy.—

Remember, have multiple steams of income that do not need you to be present for them to keep producing. To have multiple sources of income, simply desire it to be so, make it part of your goals, visualize and start buying books and magazines and talking to people. The right businesses, investments, and sources will then simply start coming to you. And always keep wise counsel for everything; have a person who understands wealth consciousness and specializes in that area to advise and counsel you. Learn also to trust your feelings, but not your emotions. Follow your desires. It is easy.

—I am wealth. I am abundance. I am joy.—

Of highest importance, remember always that the universe gives you exactly, *exactly*, what you are and think. Read this twice: If you believe that money is bad, is unworthy, is evil, is shameful, or anything else negative, and if you believe that you are none of those things yourself, you create a conflict within you. You give the universe the message that you are a "good and positive" person, and that money is a "bad and negative" thing. So, in the interests of honoring your conflicting message, the universe gives you conflicting results, and you end up with little money. You must honestly and genuinely identify your "values" with the "values" you assign to money. If you believe you are a "good" person, then truly believe that money is a "good" thing. And vice versa. Those who believe they are good people and that money is bad end up with little money. Those who believe they are bad people and that money is for good people end up with no money. Those who feel they love money and that money loves them—that it is all "good" or "bad" just as they are—are the ones who end up with it.

And always remember that, if you believe in abundance, you shall have it; if you do not, you shall not have it. You must seek to understand intricately the abundance of the universe. See it, feel it, understand it, be it. You get exactly what you think and are. To the extent that you think of and believe in shortages, you shall have them. To the extent that you think of and believe in abundance, you shall have it.

—I am wealth. I am abundance. I am joy.—

All other things held constant, to the extent that an individual or society understands and uses money in the right productive and multiplicative way, so will it have wealth and happiness.

AFTERWORD

THAT WAS A BRIEF OVERVIEW on how to handle the physical aspects of wealth consciousness. There is a lot more to know on specific aspects of money and business, depending on what your business interests are. As a start, visit *aHappyPocket.com* to find links and free resources as well. Many books have also been written worldwide on almost every current business topic, so you will never lack the information you need when it comes to handling the physical aspects of wealth. The book you are reading now was primarily to take you on a quantum leap into the source of wealth—the non-physical aspects of wealth consciousness that so many others often ignore or are unaware of. Combine this wealth-consciousness knowledge that you now have with the appropriate books and with any other information you can get your hands on regarding your chosen purpose and ventures, and you cannot possibly fail to be wealthy. It is impossible to fail.

Well, we have come full circle, and we are near the end of this journey into wealth consciousness. But this is not the end. Life is eternal and infinite. At the end of every truth is the beginning of a new truth. The quest can never end; it can only get larger and more enjoyable. This is the beginning of a new and beautiful journey for you, not the end of it. But always remember to keep balance. Balance your quest for the expansion of wealth consciousness with quests for other expansion. Enjoy life and enjoy your time here on earth. Only through balance can you find true joy and true abundance and wealth.

What are you waiting for? What's holding you back? You can be the greatest vision you have ever had of yourself. Yes, the very greatest. No matter how ridiculously great it may seem now, it is all within your easy reach. Seize the moment, Now. You have no reason to wait, and no one to blame. Be great, in whatever way you choose to be great, Now, Here!

Study Guide
for
Individuals
and
Small Groups

How to Use This Guide

This study guide can be used by individuals or small groups of people who meet together to discuss this book. The purpose of these exercises and questions is to help you reflect on how you experience what the author writes about in your daily life. It is not about simply repeating what the author wrote. Therefore, there are no right or wrong answers—only your descriptions of the experiences you have of this book in your life.

If you are an individual, consider using a journal to work through the exercises and questions that follow. If you use this study guide in a small group, make sure you have plenty of time to discuss the questions or work on the exercises so that members of the group can fully participate.

Chapter 1

Describe how "real" money is to you during your average day. How does having money in your pocket, wallet, or bank account make you feel?

Review the third paragraph on page three, continuing on page four—Gikandi's definition of a wealthy person and "wealth consciousness." Describe that which makes you wealthy. Do you have enough wealth? Where do you need more? If so, where/how will you get it?

Describe or list the material or external things that you value. Next, describe the internal, "invisible" things that you value (like relationships, feelings, spiritual practices, etc.). Describe how much of your day is invested in gaining/supporting the material things you listed and how much of your day is invested in gaining/supporting the internal things you listed. Discuss/write about whether you are happy with how you value these things during your day, and what, if anything, you'd like to change.

As you read through the book the second time, please keep your journal handy to review your initial thoughts from the exercises above, or discuss what may have changed in your responses to the exercises above as you reread the book.

Chapter 2

Describe how you are "energy" according to Gikandi's explanation of quantum physics. How do you experience energy in your daily life? Where do you have opportunities to open up more of your experience of energy (in your work, family, routine, etc.)?

Explain how Gikandi's description of quantum physics supports wealth. Include in your discussion/writing how "oneness," "consciousness," and "attention" contribute to experiencing wealth.

Describe how you experience the "Now" that Gikandi writes about. If you don't currently have this experience, write about/discuss a time in your life when you may have experienced "Now."

On page 21, Gikandi writes, "But ask yourself, what part does spirit play? What part do you play, your Self, your soul?" in the continuous creation of the universe? Describe how you see your Self living in the universe described by quantum physicists.

Briefly describe how "we are all one" (see page 26-27). Next, write about/discuss how you experience that oneness in your daily life. Describe where, with whom, in what situations/environments, do you most experience "oneness."

On page 28, Gikandi writes, "All other things held constant, to the extent that an individual or society understands what it and its universe are made of and learns how to control that creation, so will it have wealth and happiness." Describe where you "control that creation" in your daily life, including your work life, as well as your personal life. Identify those areas where you feel you have achieved some "wealth and happiness" and those areas where you would like to experience more "wealth and happiness," and how you plan to experience more.

Chapter 3

Describe how changing your mind about time—understanding that past, present and future all happen at the same time right Now—affects your daily life. Describe how changing your mind about time changes your mind about work, family, your Self, money, the world, etc. Also describe those parts of your life that need to root themselves more deeply in your new understanding of time.

On page 33, Gikandi writes, "Make an irrevocable commitment to yourself to make Now the best moment of your life ever!" Describe how you plan to do that. Be as concrete as possible. For example, "I will stop right now wishing I had a better-paying job," or "I am stopping being so hard on myself because I'm not where I think I should be in my life," or "I am telling myself 12 times a day that all I need, I already have," etc.

On page 35, Gikandi writes, "Decide right now to face every experience as new by choosing to forget that you have faced it before." List those experiences in your life, which you've encountered repeatedly over the years that you will choose to "experience as new." These may include particular relationships, an aspect of your work, your golf game, driving the car, etc. Be as specific and concrete as possible.

Identify and list your biggest daydreams—those areas of your life where you begin with "if only . . ." Describe how you will change those daydreams into opportunities to experience the Now.

List some deadlines or goals that your are facing. Choose three deadlines that you can let go of right now. Now, describe how you are letting the deadline become the Now. For example, "I will retire at 55 with $3 million" becomes "I am open to all financial and professional opportunities in my work right now." Make sure that when you restate your deadline/goal you begin with the present tense, "I am ..."

Chapter 4

Describe in detail how you "imagine your life as you wish it to be—picture perfect, with color and details in your mind ..." (page 51). Read or re-imagine what you describe three times a day.

List the number of reasons you have to "live and be wealthy" (page 53). Review these reasons three times a day.

Describe the changes you make or actions you will take based on the image of your life as you wish it to be and the reasons you have to live and be wealthy. Be specific and list what you are doing about it. This list can grow based on your daily review of your life as you imagine it.

Translate these negative thoughts into affirmative thoughts to help your imagination become reality (see page 56):

"I am not lonely anymore." "I won't be poor one day." "I am not old." "I am not unhappy." Now, continue to translate other thoughts that begin with "I am not ..." into "I am ..." statements.

Chapter 5

List at least five different ways you will begin to think about wealth so that you can experience wealth. Make sure that these thoughts complement one another and are not contradictory or at odds with one another.

Identify those areas of your life where your attitude and thinking need to change from negative to positive. List all the positive thoughts for each area, and review them daily.

List the top three questions in your life (see page 66). Review them daily until you begin to "feel" the answers. Feel free to let this list grow as necessary over time.

"It has been said that, if you do not go within, you go without" (page 68). List the obstacles you have to meditating every day. Describe how you will remove those obstacles to spend 15 minutes in meditation every day.

Chapter 6

On pages 83 and 84, Gikandi offers seven steps to creating goals and attaining them. Begin and use your Goals and Visualizations Journal to do each step as described in this chapter, or discuss these steps in your group.

Gikandi writes that "Wealth is abundance expressed" (page 92). Describe how you are wealthy right now, and identify how your experience of wealth now can bring you more wealth.

Chapter 7

Describe what it's like to "be wealth" (page 98). Be specific. For example, "I feel happy. I am accepting of all events and people. I am feel gratitude. I know where I'm going. Etc."

List a series of "I am declarations" that can lead you to "massive success" (pages 101 and 102).

On page 105, Gikandi writes, "Nothing in Now is a problem." Describe how to bring your "problems" in the Now. Start by describing your problem . . . and observe/describe what happens to that problem as you let the present moment envelope you. Alternatively, describe a time when you had an emergency, and your reactions and how your mind behaved while the emergency was happening.

Chapter 8

Describe a time when you experienced a significant achievement. Describe how that achievement began in your Self with motivation, focus, and desire. Next, describe how your Self, through things like motivation, focus, and desire, can attract wealth. Finally, describe what kind of action you can take to begin to experience wealth. See page 113.

Chapter 9

List all those areas in your life where you feel "certain." Next, list those areas in your life where you feel unsure, conflicted, or confused. Describe how Gikandi's book can help you resolve any uncertainties in order to be certain about your life. Be as specific as you can.

Describe a time in your life when "persistence paid off." Where can you apply that persistence in your life right now?

Once you have completed reading this chapter, go back through it again. Select a sentence that you can refer to daily whenever you are afraid or doubtful.

On page 122, Gikandi writes, "When in doubt, act your way into belief." Where in your personal and/or professional life do you need to "act your way into belief?" Describe the action(s) you will take.

Chapter 10

Describe how you have caused others to experience "massive" growth in their lives—especially how you've helped them to increase their "wealth and happiness." Have you, as a result of helping others, experienced an increase in wealth and/or happiness? Please describe and explain.

Describe an instance in which you have given it away first and what you got in return (see page 129).

Describe how you can help someone you work with attain greater "wealth consciousness" so that you can enjoy mutual prosperity (see pages 131-32).

Chapter 11

On page 141, Gikandi writes, "Your being wealthy already exists—scientifically and spiritually. All you need to do is shift your awareness, your consciousness, to that part of your Self that is wealthy." Describe how and where in your life you are shifting your "awareness" to the "part of your Self that is wealthy."

"Conditionality does not exist" (page 142). Describe the "conditions" in your life that you have created that keep you from experiencing wealth. Describe how you are eliminating those conditions from your life.

Describe where in your life you currently experience the "calmness" that Gikandi writes about on page 145. Describe how you can expand that calmness into other areas of your life that are not calm right now.

On page 147, Gikandi writes, "the universe always gives you what you think about most often, earnestly and with conviction." Describe how you are changing "what you think about most often, earnestly and with conviction." Review your answer/description daily for at least a month.

Chapter 12

Using as much detail as you can, describe how failure in your life has taught you how to succeed. Then describe how you can apply the lesson of failure in other parts of your life to help you enjoy success.

"Every loss has a gain, if only you accept and look into it and have patience" (page 154). Describe where in your financial life you have experienced "loss." Then describe the "gain" that came from that loss (note: the gain may or may not be financial, but may have been experienced in another part of your life).

Chapter 13

Describe why "want," according to Gikandi, will never bring you wealth. Next, describe how and where in your life you are replacing "want" with "desire" or "wish."

Describe a time in your life when you got what you "desired." Be sure to describe how desiring it felt different from wanting it. Describe how you are eliminating all forms of "want" in your life.

Chapter 14

Describe your "purpose." Be as detailed as possible, and include both your personal and professional life. Review your purpose daily, and adjust/expand as you discover more about your purpose.

Identify any area of your life that is currently not experiencing your "purpose." Describe how you are making choices, taking actions, altering your thinking, etc. to extend your purpose to that area.

Chapter 15

Describe where and how in your life you are giving.

Describe a time you were surprised to receive something after a (possibly) lengthy time of giving.

Describe how you are developing "an awareness that enables you to look out for and see all opportunities where you can give something freely and cheerfully" (page 171).

Chapter 16

Describe how experiencing "gratitude" creates wealth and then describe how you experience "gratitude" every day.

Describe how you can use gratitude in your life to "negate resistance" (page 179) to circumstances.

Chapter 17

On page 181, Gikandi writes, "Consciousness is the set of attributes and capabilities that enable you to be awake to a state of being or set of experiences." Describe where you are experiencing being conscious or awake.

Describe how and where you are deciding to be mindful and deliberate in your life (page 182).

Describe how you are building your "internal value" in your life now (see page 184). Next, describe areas of your life where you need to build more value and describe how you are doing that.

Describe other people in your personal and professional network who are "good and happy" (see page 185). Next, describe those people in your personal and professional network who need more goodness and happiness in their lives. Finally, describe how you are helping those who need more goodness and happiness, and how you are consciously building and deepening relationships with those who are good and happy.

Chapter 18

Describe where in your life you feel you "owned" or are "owned" by something/someone else. Describe how you are replacing that "ownership" with the "idea of temporary custodianship" (see page 190), and describe how this makes you feel.

Identify those past moments that you or your ego clings to. Describe how you are letting those moments go into Self (see pages 191-92).

On page 192, Gikandi asks two questions:

"Is this the greatest version of the grandest vision I have ever had of myself?"

"What would love do?"

Write these questions in your Goals and Visualizations Journal. Read and answer these questions daily. Remember to make adjustments in your life based on your answers.

Describe how you feel about "change." Then describe any adjustments you may need to make in your thinking about change.

Describe how your daily meditation is going. Be sure to describe any adjustments you need to make (time, length of meditation, place, etc.) in order to ensure that you meditate daily (see page 213).

Chapter 19

Describe how you "act from a position of Oneness" in your life (page 216). Describe where in your life you need to experience Oneness.

Describe how experiencing "custodianship" enhances Oneness in your life (see page 216).

"Harmony is extremely profitable" (page 217). Describe how harmony is profitable to you now. Next, describe where and how you are bringing harmony into your life.

Chapter 20

On page 224, Gikandi writes, "Scarcity is not real; it only appears when we choose to see it." Describe where you are choosing to see "scarcity" in your life. Then, describe how you are blinding yourself to scarcity in order to see abundance.

Describe how "competitive thinking" feeds the illusion of scarcity in your life. Next, describe how you transform competitive thinking into "creative thinking" to attract abundance in your life (page 226).

Describe any thoughts you may have that keep you from knowing that "there is an infinite source of supply" (page 227). List the steps you are taking to eliminate those thoughts.

Chapter 21

Describe the joy you are experiencing in your life right now. Also describe how you "cause another to be happy" in your life now (page 231).

"Happiness is a decision" (page 232). Describe the circumstances/experiences that brought you to make a decision to be happy.

On page 232, Gikandi writes, "... happiness comes from you making things happen for you instead of you waiting for things to happen to and for you." Describe how you are doing this in your personal and professional life.

Describe a time in your life when you found humor and it liberated you (page 234). Describe where you are looking for the humorous side of your life now.

If you have "something about yourself that you do not like," describe how you are changing that in order to like and love yourself (page 235).

Chapter 22

"Money has two primary uses: it allows us to exchange our gifts and it allows us to experience wealth" (page 247). Describe how you handle/manage money in your life—whether you are "thrifty," "generous," "fearful," "proud of it," etc. Next, describe how you use money to "exchange gifts" and "experience wealth."

On page 251, Gikandi asks, "What are you fabulous at—not just good, but fabulous?" Answer that question. Next, describe what in your personal and professional life you can delegate so that you can focus on doing whatever you do that is fabulous.

Describe how you are making your money work for you instead of you working for your money (see page 257). Describe any adjustments you need to make about how your money works for you (see especially page 258).

List all the assets in your life. Then, list all the liabilities (see pages 260-62). Describe how you are decreasing your liabilities and building your assets.

On page 263, Gikandi writes, "Say to yourself and believe it: 'Money loves me, and I love money.'" Describe how you feel about that statement. Next, describe what in your life/thinking do you need to change to make that statement comfortably (See also page 267).

ABOUT THE AUTHOR

 David Cameron Gikandi is a native of Kenya and currently lives in Mombasa. He holds a BS in International Business from Jacksonville University, Florida. He has an MS in Information Technology from Griffith University (Queensland, Australia). He is a real estate promoter and investor in Kenya. He also has an active seminar and motivational presence on the Internet. David was the Creative Consultant on "The Secret," a 2006 documentary based on Rhonda Byrne's book.

HAMPTON ROADS
PUBLISHING COMPANY

. . . for the evolving human spirit

Hampton Roads Publishing Company publishes books on a variety
of subjects, including spirituality, health, and other related topics.

For a copy of our latest trade catalog, call 978-465-0504 or visit our
distributor's website at *redwheelweiser.com*.